Beneath a Valley Sky

Beneath a Valley Sky

Bronwen Hosie

This book is dedicated to the memory of my dear brother Jonathan.

First published 2009

The History Press
The Mill, Brimscombe Port
Stroud, Gloucestershire, GL5 2QG
www.thehistorypress.co.uk

British Library Cataloguing in Publication Data.
A catalogue record for this book is available from the British Library.

ISBN 978 0 7524 5163 3

Typesetting and origination by The History Press
Printed in Great Britain

Contents

PART ONE: DAI'S STORY

PART TWO: BRONWEN'S STORY

Part One

DAI'S STORY

I

Foreign Fields

Really it was Baron Buckland who was to blame for Dai leaving the valley.

In 1922 Baron Buckland moved to Bwlch, in Brecknockshire where he became a J.P. for that county as well as for the borough of Merthyr Tydfil, which was his native town. In 1923 he was granted the freedom of the borough of Merthyr Tydfil, and was created first Baron Buckland of Bwlch in 1926.

Dai's Uncle Jim, his mother's brother, had married Aunty Mag, who had lived and grown up with her parents in Bwlch. When Dai was small, Uncle Jim and Aunty Mag lived at the top of Lady Tyler Terrace in Rhymney, but after Uncle Jim went into the army and was posted to Brecon, they moved into a house right across from the barracks.

Every so often, Uncle Jim did odd jobs for Baron Buckland. The Baron had many business connections, one of them being with Hudson & Terraplane motor cars in Chiswick; he asked Dai's uncle if he wanted to be a foreman in the factory. Uncle Jim and Aunty Mag thought this offer over and very soon moved house.

Uncle Jim was very happy working at Hudson & Terraplane, but he didn't think much of the maintenance foreman who was not a very good worker, so he asked his brother Dave if he would like a job as maintenance foreman in the factory.

His brother Dave thought this offer over and then, with his wife Florrie, moved to Hounslow where Jim and Mag were living.

Hudson & Terraplane dealt in American cars. These cars were shipped from America in bits and pieces to be assembled at the factory.

Baron Buckland. (Photograph courtesy of Merthyr Tydfil Library)

Neville Chamberlain and Baron Buckland. (Photograph courtesy of Merthyr Tydfil Library)

It so happened that shortly after Dai's Uncle Dave took the job in Chiswick, car radios started to come over from America. No-one knew much about radio in Chiswick, or even in Britain at that time.

Jim and Dave knew that Gordon Lewis, the chemist in Rhymney, knew a bit, and that young Dai knew even more because he had been studying it like a daft thing since he was a boy. So when the bosses found they had a problem finding someone to fit the radios into the cars, or repair them, Jim said,

'I do know just the bloke, my nephew Dai, in Wales. I know for a fact, that 'e will be able to fit the radios in the cars and repair them.'

Uncle Jim was told to send for Dai.

Dai, not quite eighteen years old, leaving No. 39 with love, good wishes and a hundred commands showered upon him, and with a paper-bag of sandwiches and his mother's Welsh cakes under his arm, headed to the city in England which was paved with gold, and the new life of Hudson & Terraplane.

Top left: Dai Morrissey's mother, Saranne, and his Uncle Dave.
Centre left: Dai Morrissey's mother with Pat and Cynthia (Jim and Mag's children) at Wellesley Avenue, Hounslow.
Bottom left: Pat, Dai Morrissey and Cynthia.
Top right: Dai Morrissey's Aunty Florrie, Uncle Dave's wife.
Bottom right: Dai Morrissey's Aunty Mag (In Canada in later years).

Hudson & Terraplane car. (Photograph courtesy of The Bay City Motor Company, USA) This car is the one used in the film *Public Enemies* starring Johnny Depp. The car was re-painted black for the film.

Fitting the new radios was no problem for Dai. After a few months he was allowed to test drive the new cars, which often involved picking up prospective customers to show them how good the cars were. Most of these would-be buyers were very wealthy, some of them well known celebrities of the time, who succumbed easily to Dai's valley charm.

His Uncles, Jim and Dave, always knew when Dai had just finished a test drive with a well-known celebrity. He had a grin on his face that could be seen from a mile away and wildly brandished free concert or theatre tickets in the air as he approached them.

'Who was it this time?' Jim asked his nephew on one such occasion.

'The bandleader, 'enry 'all', Dai replied and started singing 'The Teddy Bears' Picnic'.

'Too bad you didn't meet the Aga Khan when 'e bought one,' his Uncle Jim called out. Dai just laughed,

'Never mind the Aga Khan,' he replied, 'if I could give Robert Donat a test-run I might get tickets to see *That Night in London*. I do 'ear that 'e 'as been thinking about buying one of our cars. I'd rather meet a film star any day!'

It was a long time before he met Stella.

The first time was when he ran her over with his Red Panther. He had rounded a corner a bit fast and Stella, having no time to get out of the way, went down with a

Henry Hall. (Photograph courtesy of John Wright)

Stella Morrissey.

nasty bump. Dai thought he had killed her but luckily she was only bruised. She didn't think much of Dai, in spite of his genuine concern, and told him so.

The next time he saw her was a week or so later. He had been working at Hudson & Terraplane for over three years and was lying under one of the big American cars when he noticed her legs walking by. Stella was walking home from her first new job at Chiswick Products Ltd where she worked on Cherry Blossom shoe polish. She was surprised when a tousled dark-headed young man popped his head out from under the car and started talking to her in a strange accent. She recognized Dai as the wild driver who had run her over and decided, there and then, that she still didn't like him.

She kept walking but Dai was persistent and by the time he had followed her for some fifteen minutes or so, she had relented enough to agree to a date with him. Then, of course, as these things do, one date led to another.

2

The Road to Rhymney

'What is that thing down there, Dai?' Dai looked further down the road and could see nothing.

It was a beautiful evening, just turning to dusk, and Dai was feeling pleased and apprehensive at the same time. Pleased because they were on the stretch of road between Raglan and Abergavenny, and their long journey was almost at an end, apprehensive because he was worried about how his mother would take to Stella.

'What is it, Dai?' Dai looked into the distance.

'I can't see anything,' he shouted over the noise of the bike's engine, 'there is nothing there.'

'Yes, there is,' Stella shouted in his ear, 'there's a thing across the road.'

'No there's not, don't talk daft.'

'Dai,' she shouted in his ear again, this time her voice a little strange, 'you are going to 'it it if you don't stop.' Dai, a bit peeved by now, stared again into the distance. The light was fading fast and he could just make out the hedges in the shadows at the side of the road, and the mountains of Abergavenny at the end of the road, rising dark and gloomy on the horizon.

All of a sudden he heard the tail-end of a scream as Stella jumped off the bike and the Red Panther started to weave crazily from one side of the road to the other.

The A40 entering Abergavenny from the south. The prominent peak is the Sugar Loaf (596m). (Photograph courtesy of Robin Drayton)

Dai had a terrible job trying to keep his balance and regain control. More by luck than by skill he managed to bring it to a slithering halt.

Dai saw to his horror that Stella, right enough, was no longer sitting behind him. Dropping the bike with a thud, he raced back up the road.

'Stella, Stella, are you 'urt, is everything alright love?' Stella was sitting on the road. She had burnt her leg on the exhaust as she had jumped off the bike.

'I think the bottle of milk in my pocket 'as broken,' she said.

'What did you do that for?' Dai asked as he gently brushed away a few pieces of glass and patted some of the spilt milk onto her burnt calf, incredulous that she could have done such a thing and beginning to wonder what sort of a girl he was going to marry.

'You wouldn't listen,' she said pouting, 'I told you that thing was in front of us but you kept going.' Bewildered and exasperated, Dai held his head in both hands and looked towards Abergavenny.

'What thing?' he said, trying as best he could to keep his voice calm.

'That thing in front of you,' Stella insisted, pointing a tremulous finger in the same direction. At the end of the road, just before the bend, there was just enough light left for Dai to make out the foot of the mountain.
The road was completely empty, except for his bike lying sprawled across it where he had screeched to a halt.

Then it dawned on Dai. Stella had never seen a mountain before. The thing across the road that she had kept screaming about was the foot of the mountain on the road's horizon. Gently he put his arm around her, groaning inwardly. Poor Stella! How was she going to fit in with his Wales and his Welsh?

'Nice-looking girl,' Dai's mother admitted grudgingly, 'but what did 'e 'ave to pick an English girl for? There are plenty of nice Welsh girls who would 'ave 'im in a minute.' Dai's eyes pleaded with his father for support. Stella had gone to bed, exhausted after the journey, and probably the strain of meeting her future in-laws.

'She is a nice-looking girl,' Jim Morrissey said, 'nice natured as well. You'd go a long way to find a nice girl like that. She do think the world of our Dai.' His wife didn't answer; she was biting back the words 'a long way right enough, England of all places!' and thinking words that were even worse. Taking her coat off the back door where it was hanging, she threw it over her shoulders.

'I'm going out,' she said, 'for a walk.' Dai's stomach turned as the door slammed behind her. His father was standing by the fire, one arm leaning on the brass fender, the other putting a light to a Woodbine with a taper. Jim Morrissey drew deeply on the Woodbine and moving to the chair, sat down. As he looked at Dai's face he could understand what his son was going through; for hadn't the same thing happened to him with Davy Jones.

The words of Davy Jones flashed through his mind.

'Morrissey, did you say? Irish blood then!' And hadn't he been just as quick to raise his hackles.

'Aye,' he had said, cocky and proud as you like, 'what of it?' Jim Morrissey sighed and then turned to his son.

Stella Morrissey (second from left in second row) and Saranne Morrissey (second from left in front row) in group, late 1930s.

'Don't worry Dai,' he said kindly, 'these things do always take time. You will just 'ave to get on with it as best you can.' He was right, of course, and then there was the matter that nobody would talk about.

It took a long time before Saranne Morrissey's frosty politeness to Stella became more than just that; years in fact.

Dai followed his father's advice and got on with it as best he could, but sometimes it wasn't easy for him to bite his lip, or for Stella to understand what was going on.

'Why doesn't she like me?' Stella would ask, the anger in her green eyes flashing like emeralds. 'Is it because I am 'aving a baby? Is that it, Dai? I 'eard 'er calling me a "loose woman" and worse when I was upstairs last night. I can 'ear everything they say in the room downstairs; the sound comes easy through those knot-'oles in the floor.'

'It's not that love, at least it's not all that,' Dai would try to explain, 'it's something else.' But how could he explain that something else to someone not of Celtic blood when he didn't fully understand it himself, only knowing, that whatever it was, it was there, and knowing it had been ingrained into his race at the beginning and would be with them for always.

'She likes you really,' he had said lamely, 'it's just that she 'as got to get used to the fact that you are English.'

'And that I'm 'aving a baby,' Stella added. Dai sighed, thinking of how his mother had been expecting him when she married and how her father, Davy Jones, was determined that he was not going to give permission for his daughter to marry Irish Catholic blood. She had been seven months gone before her mother, Annie, had finally persuaded Davy Jones to sign the consent paper.

Of course, Stella, who young as she was, was a very practical and level-headed girl, thought the whole thing nonsense. Dai was beginning to wonder himself.

3

The Newport Trip

Dai was friendly with Granville Blunt who was the projectionist in the State cinema in Pontlottyn. As Dai hadn't seen Granville for some time, because of being in England and working with Hudson & Terraplane, now he was back visiting, he and Stella and Granville were always either in Dai's house or the State. Stella liked Granville and didn't mind Dai spending so much time with him. Dai jokingly called him 'Granville the Gooseberry'.

One Saturday, the three of them decided to go to Newport. There was just one problem. Try as they might, the three of them couldn't get onto the Red Panther. Dai soon had it figured out.

'Get on Granville,' he said, 'and Stella, you go in the 'ouse and 'ave another cup of tea. I'll be back before you know it.' So saying that, Dai roared off with Granville sitting behind him. Dropping Granville off at Tredegar, Dai turned round and made record time back to Rhymney where he shouted to Stella who had hardly had time to finish her cup of tea.

'Come on Stella, your coach is waiting.' Stella climbed onto the back of the bike and they were off, leaving a cloud of dust swirling in the street. Saranne Morrissey, looking through the window of No. 39, shook her head disapprovingly. She liked nothing to do with these new fangled gadgets.

When Dai reached Tredegar, he told Stella to look around the shops for a while. Stella had no objections to that at

Above: Granville Blunt with his wife. (Photograph courtesy of Frederick and Angela Blunt, Blackwood)

Left: Granville Blunt with his young son. (Photograph courtesy of Frederick and Angela Blunt, Blackwood)

all, especially as Dai gave her some extra cash. Granville got on the bike and off Dai went, setting his passenger down in Blackwood's main street.

'Ave a look around the shops Granville, until I get back.'

'Where's my extra money then Dai?' he asked grinning, but Dai had already waved goodbye and was on his way back to Tredegar to collect Stella. Now, there are lots of little towns and villages on the way down to Newport from Rhymney. Stella and Granville enjoyed themselves at every one of them, but Dai didn't get to see the shops, until they had all reached Newport that is.

The three of them had a great day, and when all the money was spent and the shops were closing, they headed for the Red Panther. They came home the way they had gone, the only difference being, that with the shops shut, Granville had to keep finding a pub to while away his waiting time.

Finally, Dai dropped Stella off at No. 39 and pointed his bike towards Tredegar. It seemed to take a long time before he got home with Granville.

4

Unhappy Families

On the south side of the main road in Brentford High Street was a row of shops. In the centre of these shops was an archway through which people went to get to their houses at the rear of the shops. The houses were built around a large courtyard with stone staircases leading up to them. Stella's family lived in one of these houses.

On a Friday, one cold November, Dai, wrapped up to his eyes in a warm woolen scarf, pulled in through the archway on his Red Panther. He was excited at having finished work for the day, for this Friday was very special.

It was the day before his wedding.

He smiled at the thought of the fat pay-packet he had in his pocket and of how he could buy Stella something special for the wedding. Still smiling under his scarf, he roared to the bottom of the steps on his bike and saw Stella opening the door and coming out to the top of the steps.

She shouted something and Dai waved to her. Stella waved back and kept shouting, but Dai, still having the bike's engine on, couldn't hear what she was saying. Whatever it was she looked really excited.

Just then George Smith, her father, came out and in no time at all he was shouting and waving excitedly as well, which surprised Dai because Stella's parents couldn't

A Red Panther. (Photograph courtesy of Ian Owen at *Motorbike Search Engine*)

stand him. Dai wondered what on earth they had to tell him. Then George Smith pointed. Dai looked down to where he was pointing. His bike was on fire.

Not only that, but his long woolen scarf was on fire too. Dai leapt off the bike and ran round in frantic circles trying to get the scarf off, which eventually he did. Fortunately, he didn't burn himself; the Red Panther wasn't so lucky!

It was a mass of flames. Dai watched it helplessly as it flared away to a frazzle. Someone had thought to call the fire brigade and sure enough, minutes later they arrived, clang-clang-clanging through the archway. The chief fireman scrambled out of the engine and ran over to Dai who was still looking, with a dazed expression, at his bike.

'Your bike?' the fireman asked. Dai nodded. The fireman looked at Dai's dumbfounded countenance, then at the charred skeleton of the once upon a time Red Panther, and fell into a knot of laughing.

Dai seriously thought about throttling him with the remains of his scarf which was smouldering on the ground beside him. The other firemen joined their chief and soon they were all rolling about with tears running down their rosy red cheeks.

'I haven't seen anything this funny in a long time,' the chief told Dai, struggling to regain his composure. He wiped his eyes with his sleeve. 'That will be £5,' he said holding his hand out.

'What for?' Dai asked in amazement.

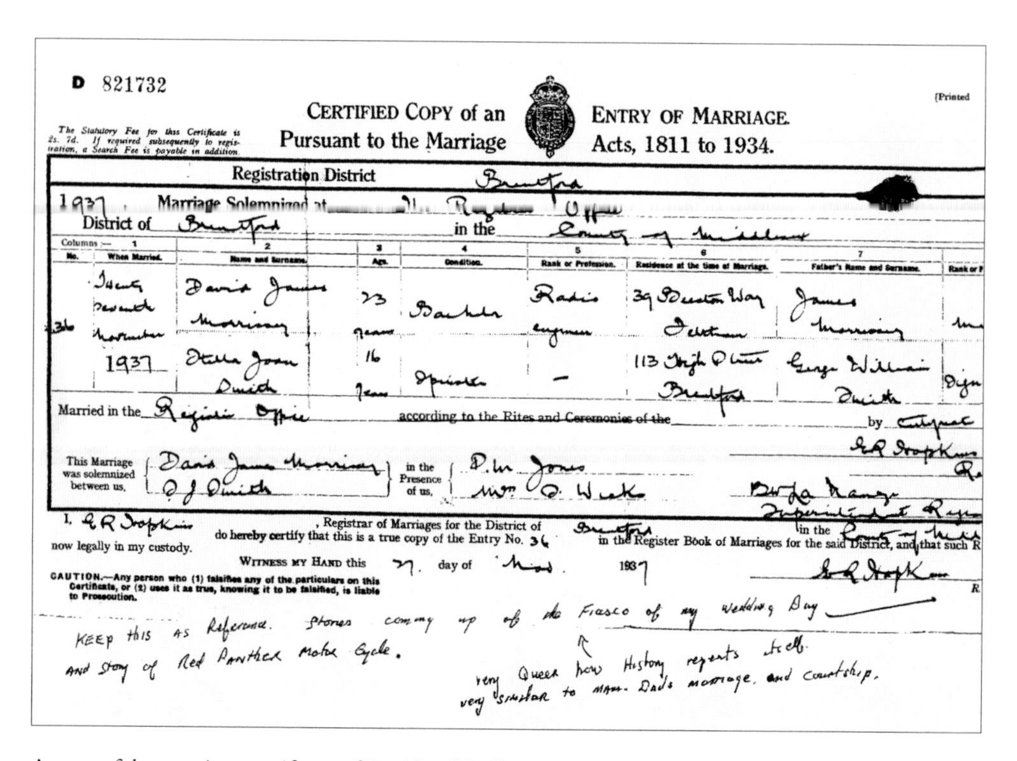

D 821732

[Printed

The Statutory Fee for this Certificate is 2s. 7d. If required subsequently to registration, a Search Fee is payable in addition.

CERTIFIED COPY of an ENTRY OF MARRIAGE.
Pursuant to the Marriage Acts, 1811 to 1934.

Registration District Brentford

1937. Marriage Solemnized at the Register Office

District of Brentford in the County of Middlesex

Columns:— 1		2	3	4	5	6	7	
No.	When Married.	Name and Surname.	Age.	Condition.	Rank or Profession.	Residence at the time of Marriage.	Father's Name and Surname.	Rank or P…
36	Twenty seventh November 1937	David James Morrissey	23 years	Bachelor	Radio engineer	39 Ruston Way Feltham	James Morrissey	…
		Stella Joan Smith	16 years	Spinster	—	113 High Street Brentford	George William Smith	…

Married in the Register Office according to the Rites and Ceremonies of the by Certificate

This Marriage was solemnized between us, David James Morrissey, S J Smith

in the Presence of us, D. M. Jones, Mrs. G. Week

E R Hopkins, Registrar

Superintendent Registrar

I, E R Hopkins, Registrar of Marriages for the District of Brentford in the County of Middlesex do hereby certify that this is a true copy of the Entry No. 36 in the Register Book of Marriages for the said District, and that such R… now legally in my custody.

Witness my Hand this 27. day of Nov. 1937

E R Hopkins, R

CAUTION.—Any person who (1) falsifies any of the particulars on this Certificate, or (2) uses it as true, knowing it to be falsified, is liable to Prosecution.

KEEP this AS Reference. Stories coming up of the Fiasco of my wedding Day
And Story of Red Panther Motor Cycle.
very Queer how History repeats itself.
very similar to Mam. Dad's marriage, and courtship.

A copy of the marriage certificate of David and Stella Morrissey in 1937. *Author's note: My father has written on it, comparing his situation with that of his parents.*

'Well, for calling the brigade out.'

'But I didn't call the brigade out,' Dai protested loudly.

'Your fire, mate.' Miserably, Dai pulled £5 out of his pay-packet. Somehow the day had lost its charm.

As if matters couldn't get worse; they did. Stella's parents wouldn't let him into their house and Stella was told to get out. It was her sixteenth birthday.

'I should do you for rape,' her mother hissed at him from the doorstep and Dai's face reddened. Stella had always looked a few years older than she was and Dai had not realised her age when they started courting - he had thought she was at least eighteen. By the time Stella told him how young she was, it was already too late.

The next day proved no better, starting with a thick pea-soup fog enveloping his flat, the high street, the whole of Brentford, where the marriage ceremony was to take place, and eventually smothering the whole of London. Dai and Stella managed to get to the registry office.

Dai's family hadn't turned up. There was no question about anyone from Stella's family being there. The smog-soaked couple waited at the steps to the registry office, stamping their feet and slapping their arms and peering into the nothingness of the street. They waited as long as possible and just as they'd decided to go ahead without Dai's family, the Welsh party arrived with Dai's mother looking as if she wished she was somewhere else instead. The marriage took place and the new Mr and Mrs Morrissey came proudly out of the building with wide smiles, as if the smog and its chill did not exist; the young couple even ignored the chill that followed behind them as Dai's mother's eyes shot arrows into the back of her new daughter-in-law's best green suit.

5

The Kidnap

Dai and Stella moved into a small flat above a fruit and vegetable shop in Bedfont, where they lived for a few months. They moved from there to a house in Feltham, where baby Brian arrived in the June along with a baby girl who, tragically, was dead on arrival. She was named Brenda.

Stella did not have any real time to grieve; she had to learn how to look after a baby. He cried a lot and it wasn't until she was in the park one day in July with her new baby that she found out why.

An old lady came up to her and asked outright what she was feeding the baby on.

'I'm feeding 'im myself,' Stella answered shyly.

'He's not getting enough,' said the old woman, 'he's still hungry, look how thin he is, poor mite.' Stella had been worrying because baby Brian did not seem to be gaining weight.

'What shall I do?' she asked in sudden panic, 'what can I do to make sure 'e's not 'ungry?'

'Top him up with bottled milk each day, that should soon make a difference.' So that's what Stella did and baby Brian was soon thriving with plump little arms and rosy pink cheeks. She felt it hard sometimes with Dai at work all day and no-one else to advise her, but got on with things uncomplainingly and as best she knew how.

Dai's mother and father and his Uncle Ivor paid them a short visit at their new house, but Saranne Morrissey hardly spoke to Stella; she spent all her time fussing over baby Brian.

Stella was relieved when their visit was over and they returned to Wales.

She was surprised some weeks later when Dai's Aunty Phyllis, his mother's sister, knocked on the door one weekend shortly after Christmas. Phyllis was years younger than Dai's mother, being just two years older than Dai.

'I am working in a big 'ouse not far away, a place called Kew, in service,' she said, 'and I thought you might find it 'andy if I come on my weekend off to give you an 'and with the baby.' Stella warily invited her in; she didn't trust the sudden change in attitude, knowing full well that Dai's mother didn't like her at all and neither did Phyllis.

True to her word Phyllis turned up once or twice every month to help out with baby Brian. Stella began to relax a little; Phyllis was really good with the baby and

Saranne and James Morrissey and Dai's Uncle Ivor pay a visit. Saranne Morrissey is in the doorway holding baby Brian. Uncle Ivor has the walking stick; Jim Morrissey is next to him. Stella is sitting on the step with her younger sister, Eileen, and Dai's dog Rex.

even helped around the house to give her some rest. One Saturday, towards the end of March, Phyllis turned up as usual. Stella was glad to see her as she hadn't been feeling very well, now being almost three months pregnant again.

'It's a lovely day,' Phyllis said, 'why don't I take the baby out to the park for an hour. You can lie down and put your feet up. You do look pasty and your legs do look awful swollen.' Stella sat down in an armchair and lifted her feet onto the small stool she had positioned nearby in order to rest her legs. She had always had trouble with her legs and had even had to wear leg irons as a child. She looked despairingly at her ankles, which were up like balloons.

'I'd like to come with you,' she said.

'Don't be daft, Stella, you won't be able to walk to the end of the road with your legs like that, let alone to the park. It will be good for the baby to get out in the fresh air for an hour, give 'im a bit of colour it will. The baby do look awful pale to me.' Stella sighed. She felt nauseous every morning and her swollen ankles hadn't helped. The baby hadn't been out much for a few weeks and there was no doubt he would enjoy an hour in the park.

'Well, 'e could do with a bit of fresh air,' she admitted.

'I'll wrap 'im up nice and warm,' Phyllis said, 'and by the time I get back the fresh air will probably make 'im want a nice nap.'

'You won't be long?'

'No, just an hour at the most. You rest up while you do 'ave the chance.'

Stella dutifully sat in the chair for an hour with her feet up on the stool but she couldn't really relax. She kept listening for the door and watching the clock. For some reason she felt really uneasy. An hour passed. After an hour and a half Stella was up at the window looking down the street to catch any sign of Phyllis and the baby. When three hours had gone by she sent a neighbour's young son to give Dai a message at work.

Dai arrived home as soon as he could. There was still no sign of Phyllis, or of baby Brian. By early evening Stella wanted to go to the police.

'I'll phone Wales,' Dai said. 'Mr 'ughes 'as got a phone in 'is 'ouse at No. 63. P'raps my Mam and Dad 'ave 'eard from Phyllis.' As Dai left the house to go to the phone box Stella sat down and began to cry.

She was at the window again in time to see him walking back to the house. His face looked like thunder.

'What's 'appened, Dai? Is Brian alright?'

''e's in Wales,' Dai blurted out. 'Phyllis took 'im to Paddington and got on the train with 'im.'

'In Wales!' Stella's voice didn't sound like her own; she couldn't believe what she was hearing. 'What do you mean, in Wales, Dai? Our baby in Wales?'

'Phyllis took 'im,' Dai repeated, ''e's with my Mam and Dad in Rhymney, at No. 39.'

'Who does that Phyllis think she is? She can't just take our baby away. Are your Mam and Dad going to bring Brian back to us, Dai? They'll 'ave to bring 'im back.' Dai was at a loss for words. He knew his mother didn't like Stella and he knew that his mother could be very determined when she set her mind to something. Dai had hoped that time would sort things out. Never, in a thousand years, would he have thought his mother could be stupid enough to get Phyllis to steal their baby.

'We'll get 'im back, love, don't you worry,' he said, seeing the panic in Stella's face. But deep inside, Dai's stomach was churning. How on earth was he going to sort this one out?

6

War and Wireless

One Friday in September, Hitler walked into Poland.

Dai was at work in Hudson & Terraplane when the announcement came over the radio. Realising that this would mean war, Dai's first thoughts were for Stella, who was eight months pregnant. Work was cancelled for the day and everyone went home to sort out things.

Dai and Stella had moved to Marina Villa, on the Imperial Road, Bedfont. Getting there as quickly as he could, and hurriedly explaining the situation, Dai got Stella to throw a few things in a case.

'Come on, Stella, 'urry up love. We can't 'ang around. I've got to get you to Paddington. There's not much light left and the station will probably be mobbed.' Stella didn't have to be told twice. For months she had been travelling from London to Wales and back again to see as much of little Brian as she could. Each time she'd tried to bring him back Dai's mother would have him whisked off smartly to a neighbour's house so that she couldn't find him.

The streets were busier than they had ever seen before and it was getting dark before they had made even half of their journey to the station. For the first time they realised what the blackout really meant.

As darkness crept in, all the street lights went out, and there were no lights on the cars and trolley buses. Dai walked into someone on a bicycle and they got lost umpteen times. At long last they reached Paddington Station to find everything in darkness except for an occasional shielded lamp.

It was very eerie when the train came in, not a light upon it, and Dai had to fight through the crowd with his young wife to get her onto the train. With a lot of elbowing, kneeing and shoving he managed to claim a seat for Stella. When Dai left her, she was sitting quietly in the darkness of a crowded carriage.

Dai watched the train as best he could as it pulled out of the station, listened to it more like. When he couldn't hear it anymore, he turned and pushed his way outside to the darkness of the streets. The journey back to Bedfont seemed to take ages but, at last, Dai made his way into the house and went straight to bed. There was no point staying up, he couldn't put the light on, not that he was in any frame of mind to do anything. All he could think of was Stella.

He didn't sleep a wink.

On the Saturday morning Dai had a quick cup of tea and made his way to Hudson & Terraplane. As he was clocking in, he noticed a note for him to report to the new manager.

'I've got a telegram for you Dai,' the manager said. Dai immediately thought of Stella. The manager, noticing his alarm, was quick to reassure him. 'Nothing personal, Dai. It's from the War Office.'

'War Office?'

'Yes, Dai. I'll read it to you, 'Report to the Royal Army Service Depot, Feltham, Middlesex. Arrive at 10a.m. Report to commanding officer, Major Beard.' Dai couldn't believe it.

'The war 'asn't started yet,' he said, 'and they're calling me up.'

'It's not quite as bad as that, Dai. You're not being called up as a soldier, but a civil servant.'

''Ow do you know that?'

'Do you remember being interviewed by a man here a few years ago, Dai?' Dai did remember. The man had been immaculately dressed in a smart pin-stripe suit, waistcoat, Albert watch, bowler hat, the lot. But that wasn't the main reason why Dai remembered him. There had been a certain air of mystery about the visit and Dai had been told by the management that on no account was he to ask any questions. It was no wonder Dai remembered.

'Aye, I remember 'im,' Dai said, 'who was 'e?'

'He was sent here to assess you and put you on a reserve list of skilled workers for the Government if the need ever arose. Well, Dai, the need has arisen. Tomorrow you have to leave here and work for the Government with the army.' Dai had no choice.

The next day, the same day that Britain and France declared war on Germany, he reported at 10a.m., precisely as instructed, to Major Beard at the Royal Army Service Depot, Feltham, where he was told he would spend the duration of the hostilities.

Dai hated the word 'hostilities', it conjured up all sorts of unpleasant images. He had a sinking feeling in the pit of his belly. He had felt this feeling before and realised that he wasn't looking forward to this job of working for the Government and he wasn't looking forward to the times ahead.

As it happened, a phoney war developed for a time, and the bombers expected every day from Germany didn't arrive.

At the end of October, Dai got Stella to come back to Bedfont with their new baby daughter, Ann, who had been born two weeks earlier in Rhymney; in the side room Dai had once used as a workshop at No. 39. Dai should have put his foot down there and then about little Brian but he didn't; not wanting an all out row with his mother and, persuading Stella that it would be easier to leave Brian with his parents, they travelled back without him. Brian stayed with his Gran and Grancher Morrissey in Forge Street, much to their delight.

Life soon slotted in to a daily routine with Dai going to the barracks every day and Stella looking after the baby. There was one consolation in being a civil servant working for the Government; Dai found that his wages were sky high. In fact, he felt like a millionaire. So, all in all, things were quite cosy. Then, one night, as he was listening to the wireless, the programme was interrupted by a special broadcast. The Air Ministry was asking urgently for volunteers with a skilled knowledge of wireless.

'That's me, Stella,' Dai said turning to his wife in surprise. 'I 'ave got a skilled knowledge of wireless.' The very next morning Dai posted a letter off to the Air Ministry explaining that he had a skilled knowledge of wireless.

In due course, he received an answer.

'Report to No. 1 recruiting centre, RAF Uxbridge for trade test, medical and interview,' it said. So Dai did. He passed the medical no bother; he did not mention the fact that he was deaf in one ear as a result of stuffing a rolled up cinema ticket in it when he was a boy.

Patiently, he joined the queue of people waiting for an interview with some top ranking officer. One of the men in the queue got right up Dai's nose! He had proper papers, he boasted, formal qualifications to show that he knew all there was to know about wireless. Dai didn't have any papers. He had studied most of his wireless books and magazines under the glow of a miner's lamp, or in the little back room of No. 39. As the know-it-all went into the interview room, Dai decided there wasn't any point in his waiting any longer and left the queue.

'Where are you going?' a complete stranger sitting on a bench asked him.

'I am going 'ome,' Dai answered; 'this is no place for the likes of me.'

'If you go home now,' the man said, 'you will be wondering for the rest of your life what would have happened. You may as well go through with it. It's nearly your turn.' Dai thought about it for a minute and returned to his place in the queue. Mr Know-it-all came out of the room smiling; his interview had not lasted long and he seemed confident that he had passed.

Dai was feeling a bit riled by the obvious cockiness of Mr Know-it-all, and by the time he was called into the interview room had worked himself up to a right paddy, having Irish blood from Merthyr Tydfil, ready to have a go at anyone who said he didn't know wireless.

The man at the table had scrambled egg on his hat and things on his arm. Dai presumed, correctly, that this was the top ranking officer. Without so much as glancing at Dai, he started the interview.

'Sit down,' he said in a la-dee-da voice, 'and draw me a circuit of an eighteen-valve heterodyne receiver.' Dai looked at him.

'Are you going to lunch soon?' Dai asked.

'No, why?' the officer replied, somewhat taken aback.

'Well, you do know damn well it will take me 'ours to draw one of them.' The officer looked at Dai properly and laughed.

'Alright,' he said, 'then draw it in sections. Start with the oscillator section.' Dai started to draw and as soon as the officer saw that Dai knew what he was on about, gave him another task, firing different questions in the meantime for good measure.

'What value condenser, at the output stage, would be in that position?' he asked pointing to the circuit.

'Ah!' Dai exclaimed. 'The trick question, is it?'

NATIONAL SERVICE (ARMED FORCES) ACT, 1939

GRADE CARD

Registration No. 7691

Mr. David J. Morrissey

whose address on his registration card is 2 Marine Villas Imperial Rd Bedfont Middx

was medically examined at

on 14 FEB 1940

and placed in

GRADE* I One

~~E.D. Until~~* (Medical Board stamp.)

Chairman of Board [illegible]

Man's Signature David J. Morrissey

*The roman numeral denoting the man's Grade (with number also spelt out) will be entered in RED ink by the Chairman himself, e.g., Grade I (one), Grade II (two) (a) (Vision). If the examination is deferred the Chairman will enter a date after the words "E.D. Until", and cross out "Grade"; alternatively, the words "E.D. Until ......" will be struck out.

N.S. 55 [P.T.O.

The National Service Act Card 1939 for David Morrissey.

'What do you mean?'

'You're trying to catch me out.' Dai protested. 'Let's get this straight. Are you asking what value would be there, or what value I would put there?'

'Is there a difference?'

'Damn right there's a difference,' Dai said, 'so make your mind up.'

'Alright,' the officer said, ignoring the cheek, and curious as to what made this young man tick. Leaning forward to take up the challenge he repeated, 'Alright, what value would be there?' Dai didn't hesitate.

'100 to 500 micro ufd.'

'Alright,' the officer said, 'leaning even further forward over the desk, 'what value would you put?'

'2000 to 5000 ufd.'

'How do you make that out?'

'Because of the reactants in the circuit at low frequencies.' The officer looked at the circuit and then he looked at Dai.

'You are a quality enthusiast,' he said, beaming from ear to ear as he mentioned his own pet topic. Well, after that the time simply flew by, and when Dai was coming out of the room a few hours later, he felt they were bosom friends.

'By the way,' his new friend called before Dai could close the door behind him, 'you've passed.'

'Passed for what?'

'Direct entry into RAF Volunteer Reserve, rank of Leading Aircraftman. Congratulations! Now go and swear your oath, get the King's shilling and that's you.'

So Dai did and that was him. It was 14 February 1940.

7

Dai the Spy

After spending some time in Morecombe weapons-training for the RAF, Dai was posted to No. 1 Signals, RAF West Drayton. This pleased him greatly as, not only was it the top signals depot of the RAF, but he wouldn't be so far away from Stella.

First, though, he was sent to RAF Manston, which was about five miles outside Margate. Dai was sorely disappointed at RAF Manston.

He considered himself a skilled worker, as he had proved time and again over the past few years, but was put on to the most menial tasks to be found, sweeping up the parade ground, peeling potatoes, doing guard duty, cleaning the toilets. Dai moaned and complained a lot but was stuck with what he was given. Later on, he found out that while he was kept occupied this way, his family and background was being vetted for security risks.

After a considerable time of gritting his teeth and getting on with it, he was transferred to the Goods Department which, at least, was a step in the right direction. His duties now were to accompany the wagons which went to Ramsgate, Margate and Broadstairs several times a day.

At the weekends, Dai was a little nonplussed. Everybody seemed to disappear, the camp becoming an almost deserted village.

'Oh, everybody lives out,' he was told on making further enquiries.

'What do you mean?' Dai asked.

'Well, they've all got flats or rooms in the town; they go home on the weekend. Why don't you live out, Dai?' Dai went straight to the Commanding Officer to check if he could live out.

'No problem,' the C.O. said.

In no time at all Dai found a room in a house in Oxford Street, Margate, and in even less time after that had transferred Stella and baby Ann from London. Well, things were looking much better.

Every day, Dai went with the wagons to Margate, usually managing to pop home for an hour or so for a nice cup of tea and some time with his wife and baby. Everything was going along nicely, until one Friday morning.

This Friday morning, Dai jumped off the wagon as usual when it got to Margate, popping home for an hour. When he returned to the pick-up point, lo and behold, the wagon wasn't there. Well, Dai knew he had to get back to the camp or he would be in trouble. He decided to walk.

As he was dressed in denims and an RAF hat, so as not to attract much attention, he walked on a farm track which ran parallel to the main road. It was a lovely day and Dai found it very pleasant wandering along the farm track and admiring the pretty little farmhouse sitting in the distance on the perimeter of the farmer's fields.

He had almost reached the camp when he noticed something coming towards him. As the something got nearer, Dai realised that it was an airman on a bicycle.

'Where are you going?' the airman asked him as he reached Dai.

'RAF Manston,' Dai replied in all innocence.

'Well then, you're the one I'm looking for. You're under arrest.' Dai couldn't believe his ears, well one of them anyway, the other having been damaged years before.

'What for?' he uttered in astonishment.

'I don't know. I was just told to arrest you.'

'Who are you then?' The airman pointed to his sleeve where he wore an arm band.

'S.P.' he answered.

'You 'aven't got any authority to arrest me,' Dai argued.

'Oh yes I have.'

'Oh no you 'aven't.' This argument, like a pantomime, could have carried on for ever. So Dai went back to the camp with him. He had never seen it so busy. It was so mobbed with sergeants and different ranking officers that Dai had to literally push himself through the crowd to get in. In the midst of all this bustle, Dai noticed his Flight Sergeant from the stores, and made his way towards him to complain about being arrested.

His Flight Sergeant and another officer were talking nineteen to the dozen in a very excited and agitated manner; it took Dai some time before he could butt in.

'Listen to me, Flight, they've arrested me.' The Flight Sergeant and the officer stopped talking and looked at Dai. The concerned look that had been on the Flight Sergeant's face went through a series of changes; Dai, to his surprise, noting particularly sorrow, horror, dread and grief.

'Oh no! Not you. Don't tell me it was you?' Flight uttered. Well, Dai had to admit that whatever it was, it was him. Only they wouldn't tell him what it was.

Dai explained, as best he could, that he had missed the wagon in Margate and decided to walk back to camp so as not to get into trouble. Flight and the officer and the rest of the occupants in the room listened in complete silence. You could have heard a pin drop. Strangely enough, Dai found this a bit disconcerting after all the noise and commotion that had been present when he came in.

'Is that it?' Flight said when Dai had finished.

'Aye,' Dai assured him, thinking it best not to mention the nice cup of tea and the pleasant hour he had spent with Stella and baby Ann. To his horror, he was dispatched from the room under armed guard and taken from one building in the camp to the next where he had to explain, all over again and again, the same story to the other occupants, who seemed to consist of smarmy looking high ranking officers sitting around tables in court martial formation.

In the meantime, Dai's friends had gone for Stella.

'It's your Dai, Stella,' they said, 'he's been arrested.'

'Arrested!' Stella exclaimed, 'What for?'

'For being a German spy.'

'That's ridiculous,' Stella laughed, daintily tossing back her thick black curls, 'you're 'aving me on.'

'No we're not, Stella, honest. Dai missed the wagon this morning and had to walk back to camp.'

'Aye,' continued another, 'and some conductress on a bus going from Margate to Canterbury saw him going through the fields and thought he looked suspicious.'

'Tell her it was a double-decker bus.'

'What difference does that make?'

'Well, that's how she saw over the hedges.'

'Anyway, she stopped the bus and phoned emergency services and now it's set the defence mechanism going and Dai is right in the middle of it.' Stella grabbed baby Ann and caught the next bus to the camp. She wasn't allowed through the gates and had to watch helplessly as Dai was still being marched under armed guard from one building to another. All sorts of terrible thoughts came into Stella's head, from jails to court martial, to Dai being shot with a white handkerchief round his eyes and a photo of her, little Brian and baby Ann clutched in his trembling hands. She started to cry as Dai came out of one building again and was being marched to the next.

Seeing Stella crying at the gates, Dai lost his temper and told the officers straight what he thought of them and their silly games, because of course, he knew that they knew that he wasn't really a German spy.

'You can't behave like that to an officer,' one of them thundered.

'Yes I can. I just 'ave,' Dai blurted out, and for this insolent insubordination was made to do the rounds again with Stella getting more and more hysterical by the minute as she held baby Ann up to the gates to get a last look at her father.

Stella and Dai Morrissey, early 1940s.

The officers were actually laughing as they had Dai taken to the prison where he was told to put his tunic on and button it up.

Dai was beginning to think they were insane enough to do anything.

'You can go home now, Taffy,' one of them said.

'What?' Dai said in disbelief.

'Home. Get on that bus and go home, out of our sight.' They had finished with their game.

When Dai got on the bus, with Stella stifling her sobs and baby Ann crying her heart out, a few officers who had boarded the same bus laughed and guffawed until the tears ran down their cheeks. Dai tried to ignore the calls of 'Dai the spy,' from that quarter as he sat there with his arm round his young wife, red in the face, and inwardly cursing bitterly the men mocking him.

On the following Monday he was posted to a new camp, RAF West Drayton, so putting Stella, baby Ann, a case and the pram on the back of a coal lorry, they moved away from Margate.

A few days later Dai heard the news. RAF Manston had been bombed, two hangars had been badly damaged and there had been casualties.

That night, sitting in a strange room, in a strange town, Dai rocked baby Ann in his arms and hummed a little Welsh lullaby. Through the window, he could see houses scattered here and there, and in the distance one or two farms with their green fields almost ripe for the harvesting, the crops swaying gently in the early evening breeze.

Dai thought of the pretty little farmhouse he had admired; it had been bombed. He thought of the officers on the bus who had mocked him and how he had cursed them. He thought of the camp at RAF Manston with all the buildings he had been marched around, now lying damaged, charred and blackened in parts. He thought of the mobbed guard room and wondered if any of the excited crowd in there that day had lived to see another, and he thought of the friends he had left behind.

In the pit of his stomach he felt an ache. He had felt this before, but this time the ache spread through his body filling his very heart and head and soul until he thought he would burst with the intensity of it. The Welsh had a name for this feeling. They called it *hiraeth*.

More than anything, more than anything in the whole wide world, Dai wanted to go home. Not this home. Not this room in England with English fields full of crops swaying in the distance. Real home.

Gently Dai got up carrying baby Ann, and went out of the room.

8

The RAF Corporal

Dai had been working on the Wellingtons with No. 20 Operational Training Unit at RAF Lossiemouth, fitting radio equipment and training the aircrew how to use them. He had lost count of the number of bases he and his men had already been sent to; no sooner had they arrived at one base and worked on the aircraft than they were uprooted and sent on to the next.

It was at Lossiemouth that he was surprised and disappointed to discover that a few of his men, grumbling that they were being over-worked and over-travelled, had started a ruse of uncoupling the sockets on the radios in the planes and recoupling them with a large wad of well-chewed gum inserted at the point of contact, to prevent them making any connection which, of course, made the plane inoperable for duty as the radios would not work. By doing this, the men hoped to be based at one place for more than a few days, or at most, a week at a time.

Dai, now a Corporal, watched in concern as the rest of his men spent hours picking away at the gum to get it removed, all the time muttering threats of what they would do to the saboteurs if they found out who they were. When the radios were vandalized a second time, Dai knew he had to do something fast. He called his group together and told the men if any of them desperately wanted a night off, just to come and speak to him quietly rather than disabling the equipment.

'I'll do my best to get a day off for you boys. Do you fancy doing anything special like?' Dai didn't get any reply that time, but over the next few days his men approached him furtively in two's or three's.

'It wasn't us, Corporal, but we were thinking a day in the town would be a break.'

'It wasn't us, Corporal, but we were thinking a night out to see a good film would be fun.'

'It wasn't us, Corporal, but we think a spot of fishing would be nice.' No sooner said than done. Dai managed to fit in all their requests.

'Right boys,' he said as they arrived at Peterhead, 'if you do want to spend the day in town, or at the cinema off you go. Those who want to go fishing come with me.' As the trawler they had boarded left Peterhead harbour, the weather promised to be as good as any day in mid-August could ever be.

Gilwern Canal. (Photograph courtesy of David Roberts, Newport)

'Not too much mackerel left now,' one of the boat's crew informed him, 'but plenty of white fish.' Dai wasn't too used to being on the water; he had canoed on the canal at Gilwern when he was a boy and had enjoyed that well enough though.

He had a feeling, a sort of sixth sense, that the two men who fancied a bit of fishing were the two troublemakers who had sabotaged the radios and he wanted an opportunity to talk things over with them.

An hour later Dai was wishing he had a seventh sense, one that warned him of sudden Scottish summer squalls. As he gripped onto the rail with all the strength he could muster, his only consolation was that the two would-be fishermen from his group looked even greener in the face than he was. Dai realised it would be a long time before they tried any more tricks to get a day off work.

A few days later he was driving through Scone on his way south when the truck in front of his came to a stuttering halt. Dai and his men decided to have a look around while the good truck went back up north to their last base to fetch the parts needed to repair the truck that had broken down.

They were a few miles outside the town but it wasn't long before a group of villagers had gathered to bring them whatever gifts they could find to thank the brave servicemen who were protecting their country. One old lady brought a basket of fresh eggs; another brought apples from her garden and cider made from the last year's batch; another whose sons were all away serving in the forces brought a home-made black pudding; an old man gave them all the pipe tobacco he had managed to save over the past few months.

They waited for a few hours for the return of the other truck, but there seemed to be no sign of it.

'You laddies will be hungry, nae doot,' said an elderly lady who looked to be in her eighties, 'I've cooked a wee drop o' good ham soup if you care to step into my kitchen.'

Her house was a very large detached Victorian villa. Dai remembered thinking that the kitchen was bigger than the whole of his parent's house back in Rhymney. The ham soup was served up to them, dish after dish, until they could eat no more and as it was getting dark by then and there was still no sign of the truck, their hostess suggested that they should all stay in her sitting room for the night.

The room was far more luxurious than the men had been used to, and even after she had wished them all a goodnight, at first they sat cautiously on the edge of chairs or perched warily on the floral cushioned window seats.

After a few hours had gone by all their reserve had vanished. Dai had managed to commandeer a large armchair close to the coal fire and was looking forward to a cosy night's sleep.

He was awakened in the early hours of the morning by a terrible smell. Within seconds he realised that one of his men had fallen asleep so close to the fire that his boot was burning.

'Open the windows,' he shouted, but none of the windows would open; they were all firmly boarded up on the outside.

Postcard of Furness Abbey.

Postcard of Kidlington High Street.

Post Card

For Correspondence | Address Only

This is the main?. Street There is a cinema in this street but its not in the photo. as you can see the Life and Traffic is amazeing you have to watch you dont get run over. We are quite Modem here. We have those thar new fangled things Moty Cars. and such like. Never have Oi seen the like before. The post office why he be older then he be. be he. come dungspreading day.

Writing on back of postcard from Dai to Stella during the Second World War.

Postcard of Church Street, Kidlington.

Post Card

For Correspondence | Address Only

Clipping Norton. Copyright.

Now lookee he heer. heer be a mighty
Boine rare busy place. Them There Telefron
and Motys. Why I remember sixty years com
Michealmess Tuesday. walking down this same
here place. Them where thar days, no Airy
planes to gad about in No Sir I say. It aint
na natural for these there young devils to fly.
No sir taint a right I say.

Writing on back of postcard from Dai to Stella during the Second World War.

Postcard of the Langdale Pikes from the river.

Postcard of Coniston Lake, village and Old Man.

Postcard of Mawgan Porth, general view.

Postcard of the village at St Mawgan.

'Open the door,' shouted someone else but the door wouldn't open either. The old lady, obviously nervous with so many strange men in the house, had locked them all in.

Dai was uneasy. It had only been twelve days since he had arrived at RAF Lossiemouth in the north of Scotland; now he and his men were almost at the other end of Britain near the south coast of England.

At Andover, with No. 43 Operational Training Unit, Dai's job was to supervise his men as they installed new radar equipment into boats. Dai didn't really know why he was feeling so apprehensive. The job entailed driving to the coast with the necessary equipment, fitting it into the boat as quickly as possible and then returning to base. They arrived at the allocated spot and the soldiers who had been travelling with them as an armed guard set up posts where they could continue to survey the area and keep on the look out for anything untoward. Dai had not worked hand in hand with the

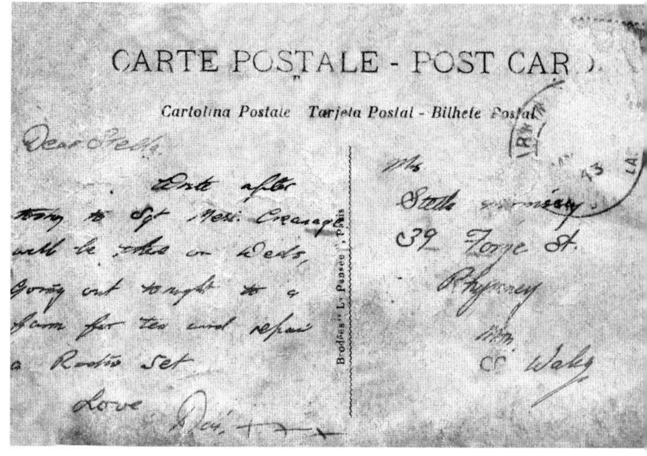

Left: Card sent to Stella from Dai during the Second World War.

Above: Writing on back of card.

army boys before, but they all seemed to know what they were doing and he was glad to have them around.

One of the vital components was missing. There was nothing for it; Dai would have to return to Andover to collect the necessary item.

'Can we come with you, Corporal?' his men asked. 'We can't do anything until we have all of the parts and we'd just be hanging around on the beach. We can have a nice cup of tea at the base.'

'You might as well,' Dai said.

'Can we come too?' a few of the army boys asked. 'We're supposed to guard you and there's not much happening here.'

'You might as well,' Dai said.

They all piled back into the trucks, leaving two of the army boys to keep an eye on the beach and the boat that was lying in the water just off-shore. It seemed no time at all before they were back with the vital component.

The boat wasn't there. The two army boys weren't there. They all looked everywhere they could think of, but there was no sign of the boat or the two men.

'They can't just 'ave disappeared,' Dai said; but they had.

9

Flight Sergeant Morrissey and the Bouncing Bomb

The following January found Dai and his men at RAF Jurby. He was relieved that they had a comfortable crossing even though the weather was cold. Dai had been sent to the Isle of Man a few times before. The last time, when the boat decided to set out, in spite of a terrible storm being forecast, he had tied himself fast to a fitting on the deck and refused to go downstairs with the rest of his men. They thought he was mad. Dai endured the storm and arrived at his destination red-cheeked, buffeted and blown. His men were squeamish for days after the journey.

No. 1 Mobile S.A.M.P. Jurby, Isle of Man, 1942.
Top row: Milton, McLellan, Brindley, Roe, Barton, Aldworth, Poulton.
Middle row: Chappell, Bailey, McLennan, Cook, Gibson, Heath.
Bottom row seated: Smith, Sgt Morrissey, Cpl McKay, Walker, Gillon.

No. 1 S.A.M.P. Isle of Man.

No. 1 S.A.M.P Ramsey, Isle of Man, 1943. Flight Sergeant Dai Morrissey is third from left seated in the back row. (Photograph courtesy of Bernard Morrissey, Merthyr Tydfil)

Postcard of Ramsey, Isle of Man. (Photograph courtesy of Ron and Mary Lace, Dunoon)

'It was terrible, Sarge, you should have seen all the vomit splashing from one wall to another; a sea of vomit. I wish I had stayed up on deck.'

It didn't take Dai, or his men, long to find their way about; especially with the fifteen bicycles he had commandeered on the island with his special security pass.

'Necessary supplies for the war effort,' he said in his new role as Flight Sergeant. They were able to reach all the outlying farms and within a few days had supplies of eggs and other farm produce being delivered by armed escort back to Uxbridge, where their friends collected the boxes of 'urgent supplies' and distributed them among the service families.

Stella, now expecting another baby, was delighted to be able to go to the Isle of Man with Dai. There seemed to be no shortage of food there; they even attended a slap up

Stella and Dai Morrissey at a dance.

Dai Morrissey in his seventies. Note the military photographs on the wall.

Radio fitted to RAF Bombers during the Second World War. (Photograph courtesy of Ray Robinson; robinson@shirk.mq.edu.au)

Radio showing internal layout.

A list of some of the RAF postings for Dai Morrissey during the Second World War.

MINISTRY OF DEFENCE
RAF Personnel Management Centre
Innsworth Gloucester GL3 1EZ

Telephone Churchdown 712612 (STD 0452) ext 7622

Your reference

TO WHOM IT MAY CONCERN

Our reference
DPM(Airmen)/104/1/M//P Man 3d(2)a

Date
September 1990

CERTIFIED TRUE STATEMENT OF SERVICE
FLIGHT SERGEANT DAVID JAMES MORRISSEY (915954)

Date of Enlistment: (For Duration of Present Emergency)	22 February 1940
Ranks	
Aircraftman II	22 February 1940
Re-classified Leading Aircraftman	23 February 1940
Corporal	1 September 1941
Sergeant	17 December 1942
Musterings	
Radio Mechanic	22 February 1940
Wireless Mechanic	3 April 1941
Postings	
1 Recruitment Centre Uxbridge	22 February 1940
Reserve	23 February 1940
1 Recruitment Centre Uxbridge	19 March 1940
7 Recruitment Centre	30 March 1940
RAF Manston	19 April 1940
10 Operational Training Unit	19 may 1940
1 Signals Depot	6 November 1940
RAF Mildenhall	2 October 1941
1 Signals Depot	Undated
RAF Boscombe Down	15 November 1941
1 Signals Depot	26 November 1941
Harwell (attachment)	19 January 1942
1 Signals Depot	Undated
27 Operational Training Unit	Undated
1 Signals Depot	19 June 1942
10 Operational Training Unit	19 June 1942
1 Signals Depot	13 July 1942
Honeybourne (attachment)	13 July 1942
1 Signals Depot	14 August 1942
20 Operational Training Unit	14 August 1942
1 Signals Depot	26 August 1942

Lancaster. (Photograph courtesy of Andrew Panton, Lincs Aviation Heritage Centre)

Lancaster. (Photograph courtesy of Andrew Panton, Lincs Aviation Heritage Centre)

dinner at the Prince of Wales' Hotel at Ramsey with soup, roast beef and vegetables, a sweet, and cheese and biscuits on the menu.

As they raised their glasses to toast the King, Dai couldn't help thinking how fortunate they were compared to others who were actually starving or living on meagre rations.

Dai was seconded to the headquarters of 26 Signals Group which had been transferred to Bomber Command the year before. The group motto was 'To link and guide'. His instructions were to convert the entire RAF Bomber Command to Modern Radio Direction Equipment; this was to include all operation squadrons and all auxiliary units.

The work was carried out at a frantic pace, everyone realising the urgency of the situation. Dai wasn't feeling happy about it.

Lancaster. (Photograph courtesy of Andrew Panton, Lincs Aviation Heritage Centre)

'Those poor dabs,' he said, speaking of the young men barely in their twenties, 'they 'aven't been given enough time to learn 'ow to use the new equipment properly. It's alright for us, we're wireless mechanics, but some of those young boys do not 'ave a clue.'

'We know that, Sarge,' someone replied, 'we're doing our best to show them how the equipment works but they're expecting to be called out at any time.'

'Well' Dai said, 'we will just 'ave to stay on the planes til the last minute to give them all the instruction we can.' So that is what Dai and his men did, jumping out of the Lancasters at the last minute as the planes were taxiing on the runway just before take-off.

Not all the planes came back. Dai found out the next day that they had been sent to bomb dams in Germany.

'Their mission was to bomb dams in Germany,' he told his men, 'with a special kind of bomb. A bouncing bomb,' he added. They all looked at him as if he had lost his senses.

IO

A Baby in Caerleon

Dai woke up that morning and thought it was still the middle of the night, with the darkness hanging heavy in every corner and seeping, grey and sly into the middle of the room, and only the sound of silence hissing softly in the Rhymney air around the house. Then he heard the muffled voices and the sound of scraping, and a few minutes later a hole of light appeared in the window. His father was grinning at him through a cloud of glass and frosty breath.

'Time to get up, Dai,' he shouted, 'there's a baby on the way.' Dai looked outside. The house was buried in snow. He and Stella, Ann, who was eight, and David, who was four, all lived across the road from his parents in Forge Street at No. 54; only Stella was at the hospital. The house they lived in, which had been built back to front, with the back doors where the front should have been, was an easy target for a record fall of

Brian Morrissey as a small boy.

Brian Morrissey aged four.

snow. Brian, who was now nine, still lived in No. 39, where he had lived since he was a small baby.

''Ow am I going to get to Caerleon in this weather?' Dai shouted, but his father had already taken his boots off in No. 39, and was bending to the flames of the fire to light a Woodbine.

'I don't know 'ow our Dai is going to get to Caerleon in this weather,' he was saying.

'Fool to try!' his wife exclaimed.

Telegraph poles! The railways weren't running and the roads had disappeared, but Dai followed the lines of the telegraph poles, his head almost level with the tops of them.

The square at Pontlottyn was empty, not a soul in sight. Dai looked into the upstairs windows of the houses which were just above his face and there they were, every disbelieving face that could scramble to a window, blowing on the glass to make

Brian with his grandfather, Jim Morrissey.

Brian with his grandfather in the back garden of No. 39 Forge Street.

A train in the heavy snowfall of 1947 in South Wales. (Photograph courtesy of Merthyr Tydfil Library)

peepholes to see a madman out in the street in the heaviest fall of snow to hit the Valleys in years.

'I'm 'aving a baby,' Dai shouted, 'in Caerleon!' holding up four fingers in his RAF woolens to show them how many children that would make. A woman at the nearest window dropped the curtain and rushed under the bed for the po.

'What the 'ell is wrong with you?' asked her husband as she gagged into it.

'That madman out there,' she gasped for breath, ''e 'eld up 'is 'and,' she wiped the tears from her eyes, 'and 'e 'as only got four fingers.' Her husband was slow to pick up on the quickness of women.

'So?'

'What do you mean so? It's obvious, i'n it? The poor dab must 'ave lost 'is thumb with frostbite and God knows what else.'

Dai carried gamely on his way, the hysterical laughing of a man, a good bass, and the screaming of a woman, a high soprano, drifting into the distance as he heaved his way up the hill and out of the village. He found another madman at New Tredegar, in the snow where the road should have been. He was on his knees digging and scuffling for all he was worth.

''Ow's it going?' Dai asked him politely.

'Alright see, butty,' the madman answered, ''ow aroo?'

'So so,' Dai said, 'I am going to 'ave a baby in Caerleon.'

'Well well,' said the man still digging wildly, 'there's nice.'

'Lost something?' asked Dai.

'Aye, butty, my jacket, and my money is in it see.'

''Ow do you know it's 'ere?'

'Oh, it's 'ere alright. I marked the spot see, right across from that old tree sticking out of the snow on the mountain over there.'

Dai looked, and sure enough, there was an old tree sticking out of the snow on the mountain, the top of the tree anyway.'

Lydia Bynon Maternity Home, 1946. (Photograph courtesy of Paul Williams, The Celtic Manor Resort, Caerleon)

'Won't it be soaked, with all this snow like?' The man laughed,

'No,' he said, 'it will be dry as a bone. I'll be quicker if you 'elp.' Dai, being a Valley man and ever willing to oblige, got down on his knees and the two of them dug and groped and scuffled in the snow until they reached something, something hard and tinny sounding.

'That's not your jacket, anyway,' Dai said.

'No,' replied the man, 'that's the bus.'

'Bus?'

'Aye, mun, my jacket is in the bus, but there's a sliding 'atch in the roof. I can get in through the top.'

Some five minutes later Dai watched the man disappearing through a hole in the snow. He was back in no time, grinning like mad, and waving his jacket to show Dai he had found it.

'That didn't take long to find,' said Dai.

'No time at all,' said the man, 'I didn't 'ave to go downstairs see, it was upstairs at the front.'

It's a long road from Rhymney to Caerleon in heavy snow.

'You can't come in and that is final. Rules is rules. Visiting time is 'alf past six.' Dai stood there for a few hopeful minutes after the door had been slammed in his face, but when there was no sign of anyone coming to open it again, he shook off the snow that had showered him from the porch roof and walked around the building until he found a window. He huffed and puffed on it until he could just scrape a little peephole in the ice and found himself looking in to the hall of Lydia Beynon Maternity Home. An angry blood-shot eye closed the peephole on the other side and he jumped back in shock, then the eye became a wagging tip of a finger and Dai knew it was the same matron who had, in one minute, chilled his bones more than hours and hours of walking from Rhymney had done, or digging for double-decker buses in New Tredegar in the heaviest fall of snow to hit the Valleys in years. Defeated, he made his way towards Newport, to end up sitting on a bench at Newport station.

'No down and outs,' shouted a railway porter in a cloud of breath, heading towards Dai with a wagging finger, but Dai could tell that his finger was more friendly.

'I'm 'aving a baby,' he explained, 'in Caerleon.'

'Oh, they won't let you in Lydia Beynon before visiting time, mun. The matron is a dragon. Where 'ave you come from, butty?'

'Rhymney.'

'Rumney, Cardiff? Well, you must be mad to travel all that distance in this weather.' Something in Dai's face must have been showing. The porter gasped, sitting down heavily on the end of the bench and making a round 'o' with his mouth. 'Not Rhymney up the Valleys?' Dai nodded. The railway porter whistled. It was a long, loud whistle.

'Duw, duw, mun!' he said, 'Duw, duw!' After the porter had recovered and stopped shaking his head he made Dai a nice cup of tea and sent him on his way back to Lydia Beynon with their post and some eggs that had been left at the station for the hospital.

'I 'ave been asked to give you these,' said Dai to the dragon, holding out his offering. She glanced momentarily at the letters, parcels and eggs. Dai saw the hesitation. 'I can collect them from the station every day if you like, the snow being what it is, and the roads being closed.'

'It is lucky for you,' she said in a clanging voice Aberdovey would have given its eye-teeth for, 'that we are in such a pickle. You can come in but you won't be able to sleep 'ere. Is that clear?' Clear as a bell.

It wasn't one baby; it was two. Stella told Dai all about it when he was allowed in the next day at visiting time.

'You had betterrrr name the wee lassie quick, Mrs Morrissey,' old Dr McNeill had said to her, 'she's a brrrave wee lassie but I dinnae think she'll be long forrrr this worrrld.' Stella had looked around in despair. She had expected one baby and thought it would be a boy, which it was. She named him Bernard after her youngest brother, although she had wanted Berwyn but couldn't say it properly with her English accent. The second baby born some twenty minutes later had caught her, and everyone else, by surprise. She had named Ann after the book, *Ann Veronica*, but no names from books sprang to mind. One of the nurses had been beside the window making a perfect hospital bed and singing softly in Welsh. She was Stella's favourite nurse. Stella had asked her what her name was.

'Bronwen,' she had replied smiling, 'it means white breast.'

'Bronwen,' Stella had repeated, to see if she could say it and gazed out of the window at the white breast of snow topping the hills.

Part Two

BRONWEN'S STORY

11

The Zinc Bath and Ghostly Faces

'There 'e is,' Dad said, and pointed towards the red brick wall of the hospital. I followed his finger with my eyes until I saw a ghost of a face smiling at me from one of the windows. My father, Dai Morrisey, wasn't smiling. 'There's Grancher, Bronwen,' Dad said, 'give 'im a wave,' and being a good girl, I waved to the white pinched face, with its cheekbones sticking out like the white razor shells I had found on the beach at Barry last summer, and the eyes like two black holes. When I waved, a skeleton's hand came out of the window and waved back at me.

'Isn't Grancher coming 'ome with us, Dad? '

'No, love,' he said, taking my hand and walking me to the car, 'but you can tell Gran you saw 'im and gave 'im a wave.'

''Ow is 'e looking?' Gran asked as soon as we walked into No. 39.

'Much the same,' Dad said, and I wanted to add my bit about how Grancher had looked like a ghost at the window and had two big black holes for eyes and a skeleton's hand, but Dad gave me that look that meant I mustn't, so I gave Gran a smile and told her that Grancher had given me a wave.

'Bloody pits!' she said quietly, and my eyes nearly popped out of my head because she had sworn in front of me and usually she only swore when she thought I couldn't hear. Not like Auntie Lil, who wasn't really my auntie, but a friend of my Mam and Dad. Every time she visited, she would take me on her lap with that tinkling laugh she had that made everyone who heard it turn and smile, and then say,

'Come on, Bronwen, say bloody, bluudeee,' looking at me as if I was a budgie in a cage, and when I said it she would laugh fit to burst. Her laugh sounded like all the church and chapel bells in Rhymney going at the same time, and Uncle Idwel would look at my father with a grin on his face, and Mam would shake her head.

'That Lil!' she would say, but in a fond sort of way to show that she wasn't really angry. Lil and Id's little girl, Enid, who was a year older than me, and looked like a china doll in her pretty clothes and with her curly hair and big baby-blue eyes would smile at me coyly from behind her mother's chair. I never heard her saying 'bloody'; not for a long time anyway.

Gran turned away from us, starting to potch about with cups and saucers and a tea caddy which had a picture of a king on one side and soldiers on the other, until Dad told her to sit down and made us all a cup of tea. Someone walked past the bailey whistling a hymn.

'Who was that, Dad?'

'Just a man, love.'

'What was 'e whistling? '

'An 'ymn, love.'

'What's that then, Dad?'

'A special song to praise God.'

'What's an undertaker, Dad?' Dad looked a bit taken aback when I squeezed in that question, sly-like, because it had nothing to do with the man whistling outside, at least I don't think it did, unless he was an undertaker.

I had heard the word from two old women who had stopped in the middle of the road for a chat the day before, the one thin and hungry looking, the other roly like my Gran, with the same bun rolled at the back of her head with a pin sticking through it, and the same tortoise-shell combs above her ears, keeping the stray hairs off her face. No doubt they thought that I was too small to pick up on their conversation.

'I 'ave 'eard,' said the one, looking at Gran's house, 'that the undertaker will 'ave to be called in soon.'

'There's awful,' said the one who looked like Gran, 'poor dab, still, 'e 'as 'ad an 'ard time of it and it will be a blessing really.' Then they started to talk about an undertaker they had known, who was called Enoch Jones and had lived in Forge Street, No. 41, two doors down from Gran, with his wife, Rowie, and his children, only they didn't live there now.

'Remember Enoch Powell?' the roly one had asked, and I wondered why old people always put a remember question in when they were talking, or an 'I remember when'.

'I remember 'im,' said the thin one, lifting her head to the sky and closing her eyes to remember the better. She had a pointy chin which seemed even sharper when she lifted her head to the sky. 'I remember 'im,' she said again, 'as if it was yesterday, because we was all Methodists in our 'ouse and my father 'elped 'im to build Bryn'yfryd. Every Sunday it was full to bursting with people and I thought the roof would fly off with the noise of the singing.'

'Well, all the chapels was like that then, that was the way of it. Not like today,' said the other, and the first one opened her eyes because the picture had gone, and shook her head sadly.

'No, not like today,' she said.

'Shame about 'is son.'

'Awful!'

'But then, there was plenty like 'im in those days. Religious see. Swore 'e wouldn't kill anyone and walked into battle with 'is rifle slung over 'is shoulder. Poor Bryn!'

'Stuck to 'is principles, see. It takes a brave man to do that. What 'appened to Enoch's daughter again?'

'Mary? Teacher.' They moved off, the thin one going up Forge Street towards the Square, the other, who looked like Gran, turning her feet towards Pontlottyn and I wondered what battle they had been talking about.

Brynhyfryd Chapel, Rhymney. (Photograph courtesy of Mr Norman Gilbert)

Forge Street neighbours during the early fifties. Back row, from left to right: Billy Smith, Jimmy Spacey, Emlyn, Doreen, Tommy Phillips, Rev Harding.

Front row, from left to right: Edie Mack, Sally, Audrey, W. Smith, Tommy James and son, Mary Ann Powell, Ted Harding. *Author's note: Apologies for some forgotten names.*

I was still waiting for Dad to answer my question.

'Why don't you wash up the dishes for Gran, love, show 'er what a clever girl you are,' he said, too quick for me. So I did, rinsing the cups and saucers in cold water from the only tap by the bosh in the corner, and Gran told me what a big girl I was and gave me a wafer biscuit from the barrel.

I sat on the floor in front of the fire, watching the flames as the biscuit melted in my mouth, thinking of the last time I had seen Grancher before he went into hospital. I had opened the door of No. 39, wondering why it had been closed. It was never locked or even pushed shut, except in the winter to keep out the cold and the sheep. Sometimes, if there was a thunderstorm, Gran used to throw the front and back doors wide open so that any fireballs could get out if they got into the house by accident.

Aunty Phyllis, who lived in Lady Tyler Terrace, No. 16, and was really my great-aunt, had told me all about the ball of fire that had gone in through a front door and out through the back of another house in Lady Tyler.

'There was this awful stink,' she said, as if she had been there herself, 'because the 'air on the dog's back 'ad been singed and it was still smoking with the dog running daft to put it out, and there was scorch marks on the good wooden table.' I wondered how a ball of fire could know which was front and which was back, and just in case there was a mix-up, I always sat well out of the way in a corner whenever I heard thunder rolling through the clouds towards Rhymney.

Lady Tyler Terrace. (Photograph courtesy of Robin Drayton)

Miners' Convalescent Home, early 1950s. (The Court Royal Hotel in Bournemouth) Jim Morrissey is eight in from the right behind the seated row.

When I stepped inside Gran's house that day, the last time I had seen Grancher before he went into hospital, straight into the room that was the kitchen and living room all rolled in to one, it was cloudy with steam. Most of it hovered over a zinc bath in the middle of the floor. Gran stood pouring hot water from a giant kettle, her brow glistening in the firelight. Grancher was sitting in the bath facing me, knees drawn up to his chest to save his feet from a scalding. His skinny chest was white, but his face, coal-scarred, was pitted with little dark specks that looked like the tiny pieces of shining jet in the brooch Gran wore in her black coat whenever she went to funerals, or to The Railway at Pontlottyn to play whist. She wore a different brooch to the British Legion.

It was the custom for miners to wash the top half first and stop for a smoke before finishing off the unmentionable half. Grancher grinned at me through the steam.

'Come in, lovely girl.' I stood at the door, unsure. Gran made my decision for me. Snatching the towel off the brass rail in front of the fire, she shut my view off with as much out-stretched arm and flannel as she could.

'Don't you dare,' she said, with that look that would have turned an army. 'This is no place for a child. Out you go until your Grancher is decent.'

'When 'ave I ever been decent, Saranne?' he laughed and his eyes peeped at me, mischievous, over the top of the towel, daring me. I turned and went out of the house. Gran wasn't the type to be defied, then or ever. Behind me I could hear Grancher coughing his lungs out, because that was what laughing did to him now.

A few weeks after Grancher had waved to me with a hand like a skeleton's, he died. I don't remember his funeral, which isn't a bit strange, as children were usually kept out of the way at such mournful ceremonies. I never even saw Grancher in his coffin, although I had seen Uncle Ivor in his when I was just four, before we moved back to Rhymney. We lived in Penywaun at that time because it was closer to Dad's work. Dad had driven us to Rhymney that day to pay his respects.

Uncle Ivor was Gran's youngest brother. He lived in a crumbling stone cottage in a terraced row of four or five houses in The Square, just around the corner from the shops. He was a short, stocky man, with broad shoulders and a face that looked like an old man's version of my cousin, Dai Eynon, Aunty Phyllis's boy, who was really my second cousin.

Each time I had seen Uncle Ivor, he had been sitting on the window ledge of one of the shops on The Square, watching the passing-by of life around him. I was fascinated by his big leg iron and giant soled leather boot and once, he had let me do up one of the buckles that had come loose on it.

When he died Gran took me to his house to pay my last respects. I wasn't sure what that meant as there didn't seem to be any money involved but there is no arguing with a Welsh gran, so I had no choice but to follow her along Forge Street to The Square. There were no carpets or rugs on the floor, not even the thick, easily cracked linoleum of the time, just bare stone slabs worn thin near the door from the feet of many a visitor.

I was taken into the other room and told in a whisper to bid my farewell. My great uncle, Ivor, was lying in the coffin which had been placed in the centre of the room allowing just enough space to walk around. For a minute I stood on tip-toe to peep over the edge of the coffin, staring with the open curiosity of a child at the parchment yellow face, sleeping yet not sleeping.

There was no fear, but the room was cold. Puzzled by the air of mystery and great occasion I sensed around me, questions whirled in my head but were not allowed to take form. Gran firmly took my shoulder and wordlessly steered me out of the room and out of the house. I had seen my first dead body.

I sat on the cobblestones outside the house for a while, following the path of a shiny black beetle meandering at my feet and prodding it gently with a piece of grass whenever it stopped, and wondered what had happened to Uncle Ivor's boots. Gran was talking in whispers to one of the neighbours,

'My Dai's youngest,' she was saying.

'God love 'er,' said the neighbour who had no teeth and heavy breasts resting ponderously on an even heavier belly. She gave me a toothless smile as I glanced up, which looked friendly enough. So I smiled back.

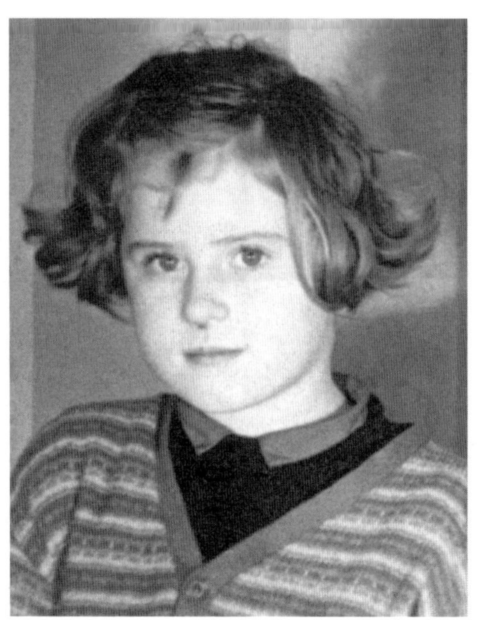

Bronwen Hosie (née Morrissey) at age seven.

12

Fool's Gold

I reached the railway lines at the bottom of the tip and followed the river down towards Pontlottyn, scrambling under the musty smelling bridges in the semi-darkness.

The river had almost dried up in places because the summer had been so hot. I looked around for a pool of water in the river that looked clean enough to splash my face with. I found a small one, the water still its usual reddish colour, and cupped my hands to throw some on my burning cheeks. The water was warm. I thought of the day before, when old Mr Owen, next door, had said to me,

'You can fry an egg on the pavement; it's so 'ot'. I had gone straight into the house to fetch an egg and cracked it onto the pavement, but it hadn't worked properly. The white had gone a bit thicker and turbid but the yolk, defying the heat of the pavement and the day, had lain there like a little golden sun resting on the softness of a milky cloud. The yolk stared at me, a stubborn bubble of yellow.

'It didn't work proper, Mr Owen' I had called to him and he said I hadn't left it long enough.

Houses in Forge Street, Nos 35, 36 and 37. Dai and Stella Morrissey at the door of No. 36, their youngest son, Jonathan and daughter, Bronwen, on the pavement. Mr Owen's house is on the right-hand side.

'No patience, merchen, that's your problem, no patience at all,' he had shouted from the darkness of his best room. I heard his leather chair creak its disapproval and out of the corner of my eye I fancied I saw the old man shaking his head sadly in the shadows.

I had done the wrong thing then! Red-faced and staring only at my own two feet, I had gone into the house leaving the egg to the fate of a stray one-eyed dog that had polished it off with relish, even trying to lick the sticky sunbeams that had slithered into the cracks in the pavement. I had watched the egg for a good five minutes and an egg shouldn't take that long to fry, even on a hot pavement.

I shook my head to forget yesterday and carry on with the day before me. Near Pontlottyn I met my friend Carole and we played together looking for soap stones in the little water that remained in the river or scrambled up to the top of the tips to slide down in clouds of killer dust, landing with our feet in the warm water. A glint caught my eye and I made my way towards the rock that was shining on the river bed.

'Carole,' I shouted, 'come and 'ave a look at this.'

'Gold!' we said in unison and made our way up the tip as fast as we could, slithering and sliding in the slag, burying our legs in the effort and digging them out again for one another, unaware of the dangers of sliding coal-dust and suffocation. We could hardly wait to get home to show our great finding. We raced up Mardy Hill, putting an extra spurt on as we passed the old stable ruins; for everyone knew they were haunted.

'Gran!' I shouted as we exploded into No. 39, 'Look what I found,' holding out the treasure and gasping for breath. 'Gold!' I exclaimed.

She hardly glanced at it.

'Fool's gold,' she said, 'it's not real gold.' It looked like gold to me. I made a sheepish exit with Carole and she made her way home to Plantation Street.

'Where 'ave you been?' my mother asked when I got in. She was the best mother in the world, with dark curly hair, and a smile so wide with the fullness of her lips that it stretched right across her face. She had the greenest eyes I had ever seen. Her name was Stella, which means 'star', and sometimes if the light shone a certain way I could see stars in her eyes.

'Every time I had a baby,' she told me once, 'some of the green went out of them.' They must have been

Stella Morrissey.

like emeralds to start with because she had already had five children, six if you counted Brian's twin sister, Brenda, who had been dead at birth.

Mam was taller than my dad, and what everyone called 'a big woman'. I told her once that if her skin was black she would have looked like a beautiful African princess, or like Ruth, in the bible picture I had, if her eyes had been brown. Mam had laughed; she was used to my fanciful ideas. Gran just called them 'nonsense'.

My brothers, my sister and I, used to tease Mam about the way she talked, because she was a Londoner and didn't know how to talk properly.

'You'll 'ave to excuse my mother,' I used to say to my friends, 'she's from London,' hoping this would explain and excuse her lack of Welshness. Still, she tried her best.

'Where 'ave you been?' she asked again, nonplussed by the habit I had of drifting off into cloud cuckoo land.

'Nowhere,' I replied, not telling her about the gold I had found, and went to my usual place in the front bedroom; sitting in the window upstairs in No. 36, looking over the roof of Marie Hughes's house to where the Duffryn used to be.

I could see it, large as life, wheel and all and thought nothing of it because I thought everyone else could see it too, so I didn't mention it to anyone. I didn't know that the pit had been abandoned and the wheel dismantled many years before.

We had moved back to Forge Street in Rhymney from Penywaun near Aberdare when I was seven because Grancher had died from the coal and Dad said we had to

Bernard and Bronwen at Llwynderi, Penywaun. Stella Morrissey is holding Bronwen. Stella's sister, Eileen, is holding Bernard.

Bernard and Bronwen at Llwynderi, Penywaun.

live nearer to Gran. Bernard and I had enjoyed the new infant school at Penywaun. It was just down the hill from our house and was near the woods, which we loved to gather bluebells from. There had been happy sports days and fancy dress parties and Eisteddfods, where I was able to wear my Welsh costume and play a triangle on stage. We lived at No. 4 Llwnderi, which was a new house on an estate. My father was allowed to rent one as a key worker in the area.

Three months after our sixth birthday the street was decorated with colourful bunting of red, white and blue. Tables were placed end to end from the beginning of the street up to the cul-de-sac at the far end and loaded with plates of various sandwiches, Welsh cakes, dainty sponge cakes, trifles, jellies, blancmanges and treats we children had never seen before. The street party was in celebration of the new queen's coronation.

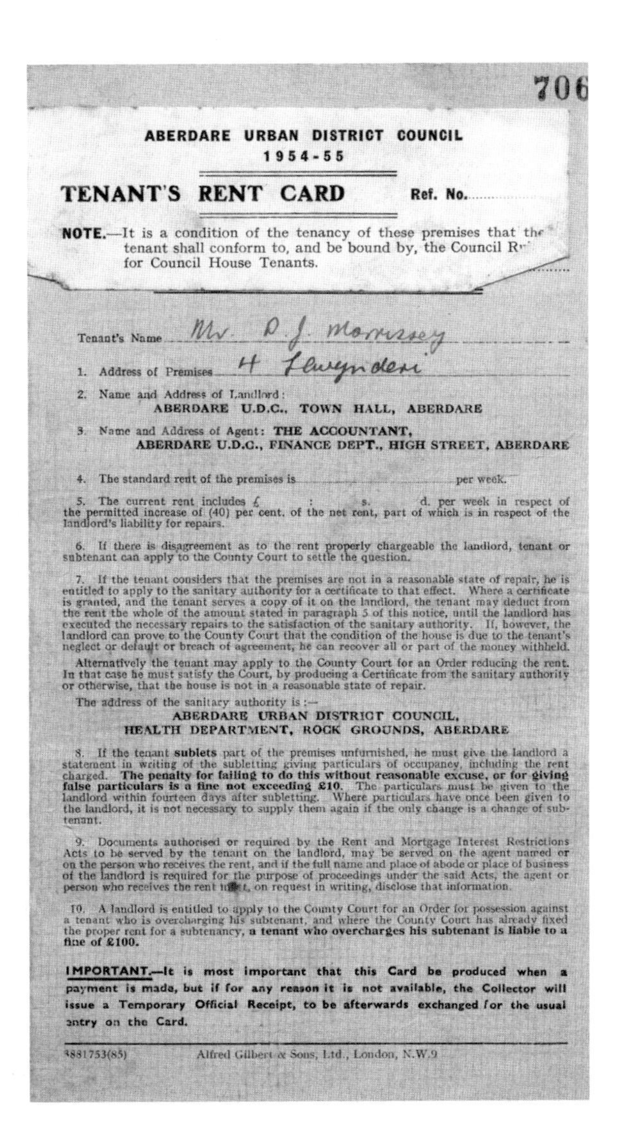

706

ABERDARE URBAN DISTRICT COUNCIL
1954-55

TENANT'S RENT CARD **Ref. No.**........

NOTE.—It is a condition of the tenancy of these premises that the tenant shall conform to, and be bound by, the Council R... for Council House Tenants.

Tenant's Name: Mr. D. J. Morrissey

1. Address of Premises: 4 Llwynderi

2. Name and Address of Landlord:
ABERDARE U.D.C., TOWN HALL, ABERDARE

3. Name and Address of Agent: **THE ACCOUNTANT, ABERDARE U.D.C., FINANCE DEPT., HIGH STREET, ABERDARE**

4. The standard rent of the premises is .... per week.

5. The current rent includes £ : s. d. per week in respect of the permitted increase of (40) per cent. of the net rent, part of which is in respect of the landlord's liability for repairs.

6. If there is disagreement as to the rent properly chargeable the landlord, tenant or subtenant can apply to the County Court to settle the question.

7. If the tenant considers that the premises are not in a reasonable state of repair, he is entitled to apply to the sanitary authority for a certificate to that effect. Where a certificate is granted, and the tenant serves a copy of it on the landlord, the tenant may deduct from the rent the whole of the amount stated in paragraph 5 of this notice, until the landlord has executed the necessary repairs to the satisfaction of the sanitary authority. If, however, the landlord can prove to the County Court that the condition of the house is due to the tenant's neglect or default or breach of agreement, he can recover all or part of the money withheld.

Alternatively the tenant may apply to the County Court for an Order reducing the rent. In that case he must satisfy the Court, by producing a Certificate from the sanitary authority or otherwise, that the house is not in a reasonable state of repair.

The address of the sanitary authority is :—
ABERDARE URBAN DISTRICT COUNCIL,
HEALTH DEPARTMENT, ROCK GROUNDS, ABERDARE

8. If the tenant **sublets** part of the premises unfurnished, he must give the landlord a statement in writing of the subletting giving particulars of occupancy, including the rent charged. **The penalty for failing to do this without reasonable excuse, or for giving false particulars is a fine not exceeding £10.** The particulars must be given to the landlord within fourteen days after subletting. Where particulars have once been given to the landlord, it is not necessary to supply them again if the only change is a change of sub-tenant.

9. Documents authorised or required by the Rent and Mortgage Interest Restrictions Acts to be served by the tenant on the landlord, may be served on the agent named or on the person who receives the rent, and if the full name and place of abode or place of business of the landlord is required for the purpose of proceedings under the said Acts, the agent or person who receives the rent must, on request in writing, disclose that information.

10. A landlord is entitled to apply to the County Court for an Order for possession against a tenant who is overcharging his subtenant, and where the County Court has already fixed the proper rent for a subtenancy, **a tenant who overcharges his subtenant is liable to a fine of £100.**

IMPORTANT.—It is most important that this Card be produced when a payment is made, but if for any reason it is not available, the Collector will issue a Temporary Official Receipt, to be afterwards exchanged for the usual entry on the Card.

3881753(85) Alfred Gilbert & Sons, Ltd., London, N.W.9

Rent card for No. 4 Llwynderi, Penywaun.

Inside our house people crammed into the living room to see the coronation on the big new television my father had set up especially for the occasion. As Queen Elizabeth II was crowned before this little Welsh audience, Bernard and I worked as hard as we could on disposing of the goodies on the tables in the street. A neighbour lifted Bernard up onto one of the tables, 'Sing us a song, lovely boy,' he said, 'sing it tidy now,' and Bernard did.

Some time after this event all the children from our school were taken up to the grass-covered coal-tip which was just around the corner from our house. We had all been given flags to wave and were told to look in the direction of the railway lines. Sure enough a train thundered past on its way from Aberdare to Hirwaun.

'Wave your flags, boys and girls. That's the Royal train,' our teachers said. We duly waved. Later that day we waved our flags again, this time at a man and woman in an open car as they were driven past us on the road beside the coal-tip.

'That's the new Queen and Prince Philip on their way to Hirwaun to get on the Royal train,' we were informed. There was no real excitement in Llwnderi after that until we helped to pack boxes for the move to Rhymney.

An old man lived at No. 38, next door to my Gran. He wasn't really that old, he just looked it to me with his thinning hair and the shaking.

''E can't 'elp shaking,' Gran had said when I asked, 'shell-shock see, from the war. There is no way 'e will ever be able to work again, poor dab. There are a lot of men like 'im and plenty more who 'ave lost an arm or a leg. Nobody do care what 'appens to the men now the war is over.'

ELECTRICAL Trades Union
Skilled Section Radio.
ABERDARE Branch No 31
Secretary G HANCOCK 42 HARRIET St TRECYON ABERDARE
BLUE SKILLED CARD starting work at Sobell Factory.

Name D. J Morrissey Branch No. 31. Weekly Contribution 1/3
Address 54 Forge St Rhymney Mon
Date of Entry Section of Trade Radio National No.

ALL CONTRIBUTIONS 1948 ARE PAYABLE IN ADVANCE

Trade Union card for Dai Morrissey.

Bernard Morrissey at age seven.

Costs relating to the buying of No. 36 Forge Street in 1954.

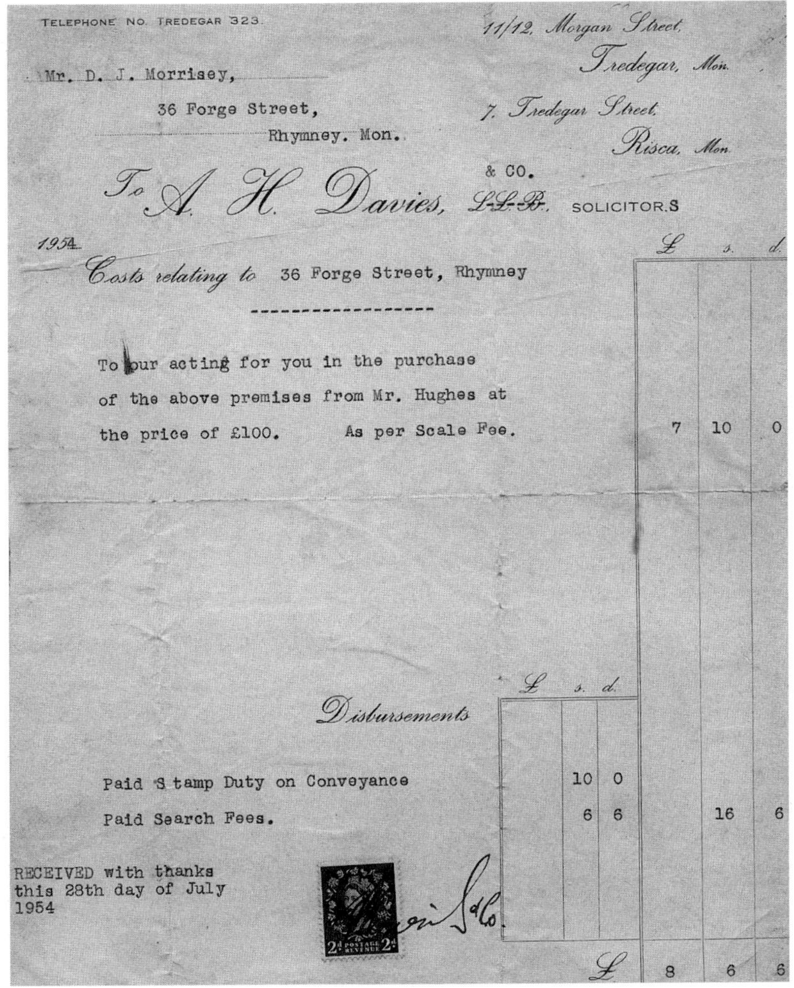

TELEPHONE No. TREDEGAR 323.

11/12, Morgan Street,
Tredegar, Mon.
7, Tredegar Street,
Risca, Mon.

Mr. D. J. Morrissey,
36 Forge Street,
Rhymney. Mon.

To A. H. Davies, ~~LL.B.~~ & CO. SOLICITORS

1954

Costs relating to 36 Forge Street, Rhymney

	£	s.	d.	£	s.	d.
To our acting for you in the purchase of the above premises from Mr. Hughes at the price of £100. As per Scale Fee.				7	10	0
Disbursements						
Paid Stamp Duty on Conveyance		10	0			
Paid Search Fees.		6	6		16	6
				£ 8	6	6

RECEIVED with thanks
this 28th day of July
1954

Stella Morrissey on right of picture taken at Sobell's Radio and Television factory at Hirwaun.

The coil winding bay at Sobell's factory, 1962. Stella Morrissey is at the bottom right of the photograph.

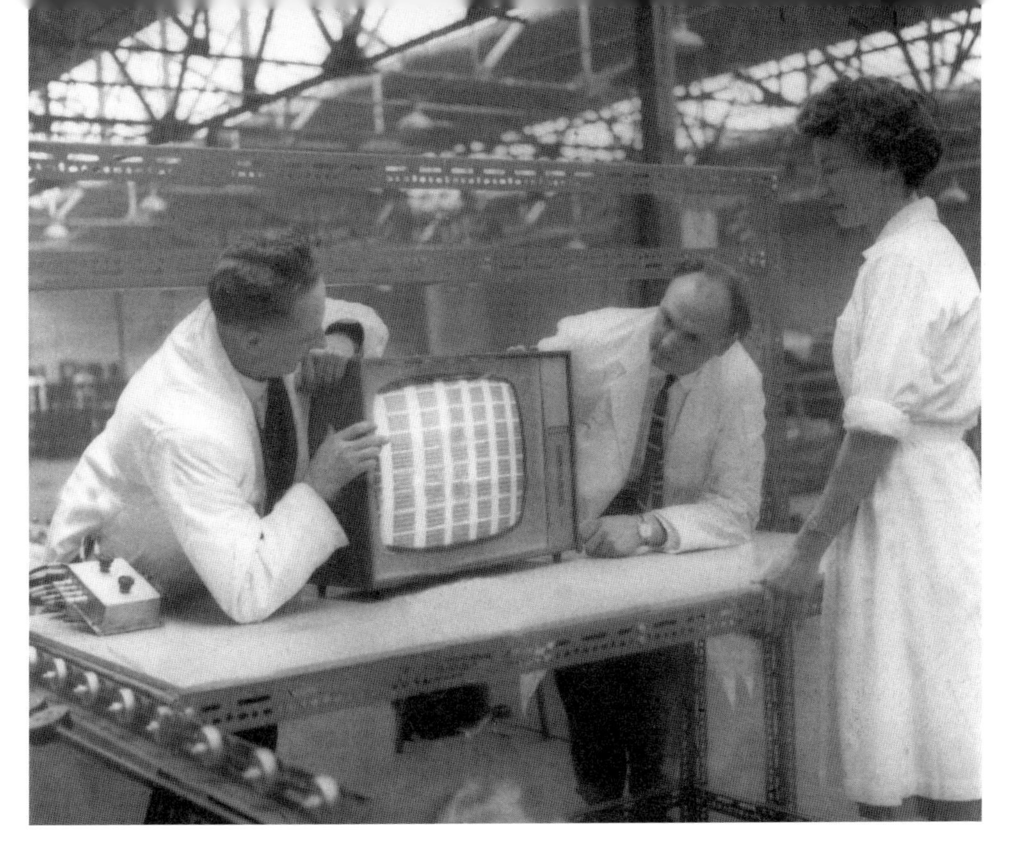

New production line in Murphy Factory. Dai Morrissey, Technical Manager on left, Wyndham Evans, Production Manager in centre, Edna Howells, Line Forewoman on right.

Stella Morrissey with friends at Sobell's. Stella is standing at the back and had just been promoted from coil-winding to Coil-Bay Inspector.

I had nodded as if I understood, but I hadn't really. It was a strange world to me with a queen and prince who had their own Royal train and a fancy posh car, a Grancher who had turned into a skeleton and died from the coal, and men who could not work because they had lost an arm or leg somewhere, or shook like jellies in a doorway.

Mam and Dad travelled across the mountain from Rhymney to Hirwaun every weekday, come sun, rain, hail or snow. When the snow was heavy they loaded the boot of the car with a blanket, a shovel, and two planks of wood. They always carried a sack of Fuller's earth so that Mam could throw some around the gear stick if the car had trouble climbing the steep hills but old BUL 668 always seemed to make it. Dad usually went in to work on Saturdays too. In the summer he sometimes drove home in a big Sobell's lorry.

On an occasional Sunday we all piled into the back of the lorry with as many friends and neighbours as possible.

'Where are we going, Dad?'

'Barry Island.' The drive to Barry was always an adventure and the day spent there always one to remember.

13

The Brass Shell-Cases

Gran had a large brass shell-case at each end of her mantelpiece. Next to these, going inwards towards the centre, were the big-sized brass candlesticks, then the medium-sized brass candlesticks, then the small brass candlesticks, then two brass boots which looked as if they had been made for the same foot, and right in the middle, a brass letter rack. In front of the fireplace was a long brass towel rail that stretched from one end of the black range across to the other.

Whenever she spread newspapers on her working table next to the china bosh and got out the Brasso and cleaning cloths, my body would sigh against its own volition. Even holding my breath didn't work, the sigh would always escape.

'I don't know what you are making a fuss about, my girl,' she would say, turning to me and tutting, 'you youngsters don't know what real work is. Now let's see 'ow good you are at polishing these, and remember, put plenty of elbow grease into it.'

'Yes Gran.' My brothers never had to clean Gran's brasses.

'Can't David or Bernard do it, Gran?' I asked once. No point mentioning Brian who was working in the Forge and came home every day, his teeth showing white through a grimy face, or my sister, Ann, who was clever and pretty and needed all her time to learn French and Latin verbs for the Girls' School at Hengoed and to sing in the Rhymney choir. I didn't know then that Ann had to do lots of jobs for Gran as well.

Gran looked at me as if I had two heads.

'Don't be daft, they're boys. Boys don't do cleaning.' The brass shell-cases were the easiest to clean. They were about 18ins tall with a diameter of about 3ins, and a smooth surface that played with my face when I looked at my reflection, making me look Chinese with their soft yellow when I pulled my eyes up at the corners.

I never knew whether to do them first or last. It was a difficult decision. If I started with the big candlesticks, which I hated cleaning, and then did the middle sized and smaller candlesticks, the lumps and bumps and curves and inaccessible folds and crannies of their ornate design tried my patience to its limit, and made my fingers so stiff and heavy with the ache in them that I felt like crying with the hurt and the unfairness of it all.

The shell-cases came as a welcome relief to my throbbing, black-streaked fingers after the hateful rubbing of infinite ins and outs. Then there was always the remotest

David, Bronwen, Ann and Bernard.

possibility that I would be called away by my mother before the brasses were finished, in which case, it was better to leave the candlesticks to the back of the table while I gratefully polished my distorted smiling Chinese image in the smooth shell-cases.

One of the shell-cases had a dent in it. It had always been there but I never mentioned it, because although it was a bit fiddly to clean, it was nothing compared to the other brasses. This one day, I did mention it.

'Gran, why is there a dent in this?' She stopped shelling the peas for a moment and looked out of the window. I looked out too but my eyes couldn't see what she was seeing. As she carried on shelling the peas, she told me the story and I gently polished the brass shell-cases as I listened.

She told me Grancher had joined the army before the First World War.
'South Wales Borderers,' she said, 'at Brecon barracks.' I remembered the barracks. Once, when Mam and Dad took Gran into a café in Brecon on a Sunday outing, she had made a big fuss because the menu said they had bread and butter and they had served us with bread and margarine. Gran had told them straight,

'If it do say butter, then we should 'ave butter, and that's all there is to it.' The woman serving us ran to a house up the street to get butter for our bread. That was the same Sunday I tore my dress climbing a barbed wire fence to get some bluebells Gran fancied. She never paid any regard to road signs or difficult-to-get-to places where bluebells were concerned. They were there to be picked and that's all there was to it. Anyway, the South Wales Borderers was an infantry regiment, and Grancher joined them in Brecon.

'Well,' said Gran, and I was quietly delighted because she stopped shelling the peas, wiped her hands on her pinny, and sat down on a stool by the table, 'during the war, Grancher fired them shells in Flanders.' We both looked hard at the shell-cases for a minute as if waiting for them to say something, and I stopped polishing.

'The first war I do mean' continued Gran, 'not the second. That was the one your dad was in. Grancher kept these cases to bring 'ome as a souvenir. So when the time for 'is next furlough came round, furloughs they called them in those days, not 'olidays, 'e packed them in 'is 'aversack, set it comfortable on 'is back and started the first part of 'is journey 'ome. Unbeknowns to 'im, a German sniper was 'iding in the trees and 'e set your poor Grancher in 'is sights.'

'What 'appened then Gran?'

'Well, the sniper fired, didn't 'e, and 'it 'is target.'

'Was Grancher shot then Gran?' I gasped.

' 'it 'im right in the middle of 'is back,' she replied.

'Was 'e 'urt bad Gran? What did 'e do then?'

''ang on now, I was just coming to that. Grancher rolled for cover, didn't 'e, and when 'e thought it was safe 'e picked 'imself up, all shaken like, but still in one piece. 'E felt 'is back all over and there was not a bullet 'ole to be found.' Gran stopped, looking at me as if to dare me to defy what she had said, but this story was too good to mess up with my usual cheek and interruptions.

''ow is that Gran?' I asked, mouth hanging open a bit for extra persuasion. Gran paused for effect, leaning forward to confide in a whisper. 'The bullet 'ad 'it one of the shell cases see, and it saved 'is life.'

Gran took so long to tell me this story that I was rescued from the rest of the brasses by my mother's sweet voice calling me to go to the shop for her.

'Got to go Gran,' I shouted, running out of the house, 'thanks for the story.' She shouted something after me but I was already racing to No. 36, and couldn't quite make it out, something about rugger I think. I ran to the shop in glee, clutching the shopping list tight in my hand and ducking below the bailey wall as I passed No. 39.

Sam and Florrie Eynon's shop, No. 45, was just a short way down the street. It was an ordinary house like the rest, but one of their front rooms had been converted. There was a counter, shelves at the back wall and a corner for fruit and vegetables. The front window held a mass of colour, which was mainly made up of sweets, with an occasional orange or banana balanced here and there for extra effect.

The open front door showed a long dark passage, a faded path worn by constant customers in the centre of the brown linoleum. On the left of the passage was a door to a secret private room, on the right, the entrance to the room which was the shop. At the far end of the passage another secret door led to the private life of Sam and Florrie Eynon. Florrie, or Sam, or both, stood behind the counter. The other side left a small narrow space for customers. The shop was full with three customers and a toddler busy slurping a licorice lace.

A diagram of the shell-cases drawn by Dai Morrissey.

Pushing my way through the adults I reached the orange crate and stood on it. Behind the crate was a wooden trellised partition separating the window display from the rest of the shop. By standing on the crate, I could just peep over the top of the partition to survey the goods in the window. The adults patiently took their turn exchanging gossip for gossip as they waited or were being served. It was the custom for children to queue up for a place on the orange crate. We couldn't climb up two at a time; Florrie Eynon would shoot us a sharp glance over the rims of her glasses if the partition wobbled and tell us to wait in the dark passage outside.

On a really hot day the display would be completely covered with thick blue paper from the apple boxes and a few dead wasps, or occasional emerald blue-bottle. This day the sun hadn't been strong enough to warrant such drastic measures. Still clutching my shopping list and holding the pointed tops of the latticed partition, I entered my own variegated world of sugared paradise.

Lemon sherbet, a full open box of it lying like desert sand; wet the finger, dip and slow suck and I would be left with a finger the colour of a springtime daffodil. Next to that the strawberry sherbet which would leave a rose-coloured finger, but the mixed sherbet sparkling in its box with its coloured grains of granules left a finger rainbowed for days at a time. There were licorice allsorts fighting for room in their box, comfits which could paint my lips red, cherry lips, dolly mixtures in pastel shades, sugar-dressed jellies to be sucked naked then chewed, jelly babies, blacks to be coveted, sweets of white, red, yellow, orange, white chocolate buttons and others pebbled with rainbow dash, sticky lemon drops that hissed through the lips, the salivered melting of sugar-icing coated bon-bons.

'Right then, Bronwen, what can we do for you lovely?' Back to reality and the crushed list handed over the counter.

'On Mam's bill, please, Sam.' Each item carefully placed on the counter to be reckoned in the bill book.

'That's everything Bronwen.'

'And two ounces of sweets please.' Another look at the list.

'Are you sure?'

'Mam said I could.' A definite nod of the head at this point would always win him over. Florrie was not so easy.

'Liquorice comfits please, on the bill.' What a magic world this was that needed no money.

The next day I couldn't go to the park with my friends. Not that the sweets had anything to do with it; I had to stay to finish Gran's brasses.

14

Welsh Ponies and Painted Kittens

Just as the summers always seemed to be hot, the winters always seemed to be blessed with a heavy fall of snow. The sheep, in ones and twos, foraged the baileys and the bins, their torn coats hanging with icicles. Sometimes a sturdy ram would appear, coiled horns heavy on his solid head, yellow eyes defiant in his search for food. The ewes, normally cheeky, were downright brazen in his presence, heads down to butt, hooves tapping the frozen ground.

The ponies came in larger groups. Hoof-beats deadened by the snow, they moved silently down the street like some ghostly equine procession. The stallion took the lead, ears pricked, nostrils wide and steaming, and white-rimmed eyes rolling wildly as he shook his head. His wives and children followed on, less nervous, confident in his strength and power to protect.

As soon as they were seen in the distance, we children raced into our houses to raid the cupboards. The sheep were always scrounging but the proud ponies were another matter. If they had come down from the hills it was because they needed our help. We clutched our crusts of bread and potato peelings tightly to our chests as we hid behind the bailey walls. As soon as the stallion had passed us by, we stood up to fling our offerings over the wall, and then ducked quietly down again. While the mares and last summer's foals rooted in the snow for food, the stallion would stand patiently for a few minutes, then toss his mane and whinnying softly, carry on with his ghostly walk. We would watch until they disappeared.

One very cold winter I struggled through the deep snow in the street to reach Gran's house. My father had already gone down early that morning to clear her path, not for Gran to come out, as she seldom came out in winter except to come to our house on Christmas day, but for visitors to get in.

'Want anything from the shop, Gran?' I was hoping she did. She looked up from the steaming kettle she was lifting off the fire and shook her head.

'Nice cup of tea going if you do want one.'

'Any biscuits?'

'In the barrel.' I brought an extra cup and saucer from the pantry, blue willow pattern, and set them on the tablecloth next to hers. The biscuit barrel lived on the end of the Welsh dresser which filled one wall of the room, corner to back door, floor to beamed ceiling. The barrel's rich wood matched that of the dresser and its brass front plate, lid and handle matched the gleaming brass handles on the dresser's drawers and cupboards. The dresser's mirrors reflected everything that stood on or before it. I didn't like the mirror above the barrel, it had a yellow film of age on it and distorted the truth, not in the playful way the shell-cases did, but in a snide, spiteful image that showed you a somebody who was you, but not quite you.

The barrel always had biscuits in it, unlike our house where the packets were ripped open on the table and the biscuits wolfed in minutes. My mother usually bought Marie biscuits. I was an expert at dunking them in my tea and removing them at that precise moment when they were gloriously soggy but not quite soggy enough to disintegrate in to gooey conglomerate at the bottom of the cup. Gran had plain biscuits too, but more often than not, she had custard creams and melt-in-the-mouth wafers, pink ones and cream. As I drank my tea and dunked my biscuits I casually brought up the subject on my mind.

'All the kids are using sledges in Lady Tyler.' I was, of course, using the word 'sledges' metaphorically. Some of them were using cardboard boxes, not too bad on the coal tips in summer, but very short-lived on wet snow. Others were using one form of bogey or other, but the ones who broke all speed records were using trays, hot from the kitchen. Gran had two trays sitting on her table next to the bosh. I gazed at them longingly.

'More fool them,' she said, 'someone's going to come a cropper at the bottom when they do 'it the Square.' So it was a no-goer then. I scraped my chair back and cleared the table. As I rinsed the cups and saucers I stared wistfully at the trays. One was an old metal tray, already buckled, the painted kittens on it chipped here and there. The other was Gran's best tray for visitors, shining silver, engraved with fancy patterns, the edge all scalloped like a paper doily. I dried the dishes and put everything back in its place.

'Thanks for the tea Gran.'

'Go on then, take it, but don't come crying to me if you break a leg or you kill yourself.'

'Oh thanks Gran.' As she stoked the fire, I grabbed my tray and raced out of the house along to Lady Tyler as fast as the snow would allow me.

It seemed to take forever but at last I stood proudly in the centre of a group of children, right at the top of Lady Tyler at the high wall that sealed the end of the street. The wall had been built on and around the old cottages which had stood there for years. I suppose they must still be standing there in their concrete tomb.

'Come and see Bronwen's tray, it's a beauty!' With false modesty I brushed aside the compliments as I set the tray on the ground. The reflection as the sun hit the silver nearly blinded my eyes, but nevertheless I sat proudly on the centre of it and held my legs out straight. A shove from behind and I was away, struggling to keep in the middle of the road where the snow was flat, hard-pressed and glistening. If I'd landed in one of the deep mounds of snow piled high at the pavement's edge, I would have died the death. I reached the bottom in record time and, exhilarated, swung to a stop just before the railings. No-one would be able to beat that time.

'Duw, mun, did you see that go? Like a bird it was.' Dai Eynon, my cousin, had been one of the first to reach me.

'Like a silver bird, Dai,' I said. I picked up the tray and looked at it.
It now had more bumps and buckles than the kitten one. Gran would kill me but it had been worth it. Full of my own glory I let everyone else have a go and spent another glorious hour on it myself. In for a penny in for a pound… as Gran would say.

15

Old Man Owen

Old man Owen had a small patch of front garden, only we called it a bailey. It was made up of two patches of rough clumpy grass with a grey concrete path cutting rudely through the middle down to the gate. He didn't have a gate though; just a space to walk through.

We all had baileys on the one side of Forge Street, all knitted together with the same grey stone like so many cattle pens laid out at auction, our own property to do with as we pleased. Not that we did much. Most of us were content with two square patches of rough clumpy grass and the grey path in the middle. We didn't even have to cut the grass, the sheep came down from the hills and did that, and sometimes the ponies would leave their droppings in the bailey instead of on the road, which made it easy for me to scoop them up with a shovel and put in a bucket for Gran to spread on her back garden where her tulips were tucked away. More often than not, I had enough

The trellis in the back garden of No. 36 Forge Street, Rhymney. The cat is Tiger and the dog is Judy.

to spread round the bottom of the trellis in our back at No. 36, where Mam grew her sweet peas.

It was a pleasant arrangement all round. In the summer, the tops of the bailey walls served nicely as sun-beds for anyone still young enough or fit enough to climb onto them, the older folk preferring to sit more dignified on straight backed wooden chairs or three legged stools carried out from the house and set unevenly on the grass.

Old man Owen had a special chair. It lived just inside his front door between the old grandfather clock that lolled against the wall and the heavy oak sideboard that was dark with age and smelt of beeswax. The room was always gloomy and foreboding, even on the hottest of days, and each time he sent me in to fetch the chair I shivered involuntarily at the sudden change in atmosphere.

'Now then, merchen,' he would shout from the bailey, 'carry it careful, there's a good girl.' His chair was wooden and straight-backed like the rest but it was upholstered, which was the difference, and in the shiniest of green leather studded with brass buttons. Aware of its status, it refused to sit on the grass, but chose to sit squarely before the front door in the centre of the concrete path. There, old man Owen would sit, puffing away at his pipe and watching the world go by.

A slow world it was too, one bus every hour; the stray dog, blind in one eye; an occasional outsider on his way to another village, head down, walking furtive through a street not his own; a ragged sheep trailing its own matted flea carpet; Forge Street children clutching thrupenny bits or shopping lists on their way to Sam and Florrie Eynon's shop of sweet and plenty.

The houses on the other side of the street were less fortunate, having been built back to front by mistake. The architect, poor dab, took his own life as penance, or so the story goes. I had lived in one of these houses, No. 54, until I was a year old. Then Mam and Dad had moved to Penywaun to be closer to Dad's work at Sobell's factory.

Instead of the communal row of wall-hemmed gardens resting sleepy in the sun, across the street had to step off the pavement and climb down stone steps to the ignominy of their own back door, which had to be their front door because of the poor architect. While we stared lazily up to Heaven, they stepped warily down to Hell.

Old man Owen's head would nod in silent amusement at the follies of man each time across the road unfortunates passed by. His pipe would smoke galloping messages up and ever upwards while his twinkling eyes followed them to the precipice and his eyelids dropped a step each time they did.

When I was ten my sister got married and moved in next door to become the old man's lodger, taking her husband with her, of course. As a result of this newly-formed relationship, I now assumed the right to enter further into the house.

The best room still welcomed me coldly, but the kitchen liked me well enough. Seven or eight swift paces had me through the best room and stepping into the kitchen where I made straight for my favourite seat. The brown leather chaise-longue, cracked and lined with age, let out a long-suffering sigh each time I sat on it, and to be fair, I suppose I was no lightweight even in those days. I tried to repay the service by stuffing back the escaping horse-hairs through the worn seams.

The back garden of No. 39 Forge Street, Rhymney. The group of five children is Brian, David, Ann, Bernard and Bronwen (the twins).

The couch, as I called it, chaise-longue's not having been introduced to my vocabulary at this stage, seemed to enjoy my company in spite of its huffing and puffing with every fidgety move I made. I loved the smell of years of lavender wax leaking from its leather. Next to the couch stood the black-leaded range which always had a fire lit whatever the weather. The range had no brass to reflect the fire's warmth, like my Gran's, and no ornaments sitting above to befriend it; not even a candlestick or clock. Its only companion was a big black kettle which sat at the edge of the coals, whistling softly to itself. The kitchen led to the pantry, the pantry to the back door, and the door to the back garden which was a wilderness.

I never set foot in his back garden. I had peeped through the fence once from my own garden at No. 36 when I'd heard old man Owen going up the back to the toilet. The bamboo and weeds had been too thick for me to see anything and I wondered how he found the path, if there was one, and how he found his way back home again. It was an eerie garden, made for the dead and dying, not for children, and I wanted nothing to do with it. I heard someone say that old man Owen was in his second childhood, and I hoped the garden didn't frighten him the way it frightened me.

16

Cat's Eyes

'What colour are my eyes, Mam?'

'Well,' she would say, tilting her head to one side like a pigeon, more like a dove really because she had a gentle way about her, and looking me full in the face. 'There is a lot of green in them,' which she was bound to say, her eyes being green as emeralds, albeit a bit washed out with children.

'What colour are my eyes, Dad?'

'Well, love, let me 'ave a look,' and after he had looked, turning me this way to the light coming through the window, and that way under the light pulsing down from the bulb hanging from the middle of the kitchen ceiling, only it wasn't quite the middle because the room had a funny shape to it, he would frown and shrug his shoulders.

'Well, to tell you the truth, it is 'ard to say. There is some green and a bit of grey.' My big brother, Brian, who lived at No. 39 with Gran, told me they might be hazel, but Gran said there was too much green.

'Like cat's eyes,' she added in a way which left me wondering if she really liked cats or not, even though she had an old white scrawny one to catch the mice in the pantry; it was blind in one eye like the stray dog, and blue in the other.

'Your cat 'as got a blue eye, Gran.' She gave me that look, the one I always got when I tried to come back with a clever answer. It wasn't meant to be a clever answer, but just what had come into my head.

'Well, p'raps, Miss Smartie Pants, the other one was green,' she said, hissing a bit at my lack of respect. Aunty Phyllis couldn't see what all the fuss was about.

'You should be grateful,' she said, nodding her square face at me and wagging her finger so close to the eyes in question that I stepped back in alarm, 'you should be grateful, Bronwen Morrissey, that you 'ave got eyes to see.' A big woman, Aunty Phyllis; not tall, but big.

'Aye,' said Gran, who had pale blue eyes and a brown spot in one where she had been hit with a pellet from a rifle when she was a little girl, adding her penny-hapeth. I bowed my head in shame at the sin of my vanity, when, suddenly, a framed embroidery I had seen on the wall of a house in Tonypandy leapt into my mind. '*I grumbled*,' it said, throwing out its words in a challenge of brilliant colours to all who glanced at it, which was every person who entered the house because it had a sort of way of drawing everyone's attention to its four-cornered world, above the single faded tapestry chair that no-one ever sat on, '*that I had no shoes,*' everyone paused, then read on with bated breath, '*then I met a man who had no feet.*'

Mam and Dad took me to that house every year or so to collect the clothes that the family's two daughters had grown out of, my own sister being eight years older than me, of more graceful form, and not the ideal donor in the way of passing down clothes.

Very pretty they were too, the clothes that is, for I can't remember the daughters, although they must have looked alright or I would have remembered. All the time I stood there in the room in Tonypandy being stripped and dressed and twirled this way and that, in broderie anglaise, and taffeta, satin and printed cottons, on the table, surrounded by 'oohs,' and 'aahs', and 'there's lovely's' with my mother trying to straighten my pigeon toes as I was twirled, I wondered who had done the embroidery and where they had met the man with no feet. I had seen a man with one leg some years before, when I was still living in Penywaun, and pointed to him in great concern.

'Look, Dad, look! There is a man with 'is leg missing. Do 'e know it is missing, Dad? Shall we tell 'im?' Even as I spoke, the man with the leg missing changed the colour on his face to a chalky white and my father changed the colour on his face to a deep shade of red.

He picked me up, packed me under his arm and did a half-jog down Llwynderi with me, my father that is, for I don't think the man with one leg could have done a jog, not even a half-jog, although I suppose that might make sense in a funny sort of way. As my father half-jogged off, I protested loudly all the while, always being slow to take the hint, that someone should tell the poor man that he had lost a leg. Thinking back on it, I think Mam and Dad really took me to Tonypandy for the lesson in morality. Heavy the philosophy in Tonypandy.

Bernard had told me once that he liked the orange ring I had around each pupil, but it was alright for him, because his eyes were as blue as the sky with not a touch of muddle about their colour. I had to go through my days not knowing what colour my eyes were really, and casting shy glances at my twin's honest blues, and envious glances at everyone else's.

My twin, Bernard, had inconveniently fallen ill at our ninth birthday party. While I sat on the bottom stair in our front room at No. 36, nonchalantly tucking in to a huge bowl of jelly and blancmange while our friends played party games, the doctor, in the best room, was trying to find the cause of Bernard's soaring temperature. Before I even realised what was happening he was whisked away to hospital, neither of us knowing that it would be four years before we would be allowed to be in the same room together again.

With Bernard, my constant companion, away, I suddenly wanted to be like my cousin Sheila, Aunty Phyllis's girl, who was my second cousin really, because she had smooth fair hair that shone honey, saffron, sandy, blonde-gold when the sun touched it and brown eyes the same colour as a camel's I had seen at Bristol zoo, and a good Welsh singing voice.

Sandbrook House, Merthyr Tydfil.

A nurse with Bernard at Sandbrook House, Merthyr Tydfil.

Children, nurses and matron at Sandbrook House, Merthyr Tydfil. Bernard is second from the left in the middle row.

I had a tawny nest for hair, attacked and pinned down on one side with a clip in desperation by my mother, and eyes that no-one could ever give a definite colour to. The voice I am ashamed to mention.

Sheila had a gang, a following of loyal and adoring girls who trailed behind her everywhere she went, offering her the best cigarette stubs they found in the gutters, laughing hysterically at every joke she made, nodding instant vigorous agreement, and hanging upon every sacred word she uttered; or so it seemed to me.

No wonder then, that one hot, hot summer, for the summers then were always more than hot, I felt myself exploding to bits inside with the tingling thrill, heady excitement and bursting pride of being invited to go with Sheila for a wander.

'You can come if you like,' she said, and I saw the light in her camel's eyes dancing and the secret promises of adventure in her smile.

'I shall follow you to the ends of the earth,' a distant voice said inside my head, 'I shall be a brave Amazon and you shall be our golden-headed goddess, I shall…'

'Well?' she asked, looking at me as if I came from another world.

'Okay.' I replied, looking around in panic for something clever to say, something she would note to mark me apart from the others, something that would relate to her, in mysterious undertones, the fact that I was a very special being, destined for…

The moment had gone. I ran as fast as I could to catch up with them. We ended up at the Dingle. The Dingle lies in a shady nook over the mountain moorlands of Cefn Golau, between Rhymney and Tredegar. Some people call it the Fairy Glen.

By the time we reached the Dingle, the sun had claimed the sky and was showing itself off in such a blaze of heat that the sheep were gasping for air in the shadows of rocks. The ponies, leaning hard into any sparse vegetation that would take their weight, were sleeping with open eyes, dreaming of cooler days, the nerves on their silken flanks twitching spasmodically with a life of their own at the tickling footfalls of flies and spiteful nips of the gnats.

There were boys in the Dingle. We had heard their shouts and yells as we clambered over the clumps of reeds and pitted grass at the top of the Common; a haze of racket had hung in the air, reverberating through the sky along with the simmering shimmer of the sun. They had stripped to the waist and were splashing about in the shallow pool at the foot of the Dingle.

Sheila stood, straight and slender and proud, like some Red Indian chief's daughter on the ridge of a sun-baked precipice, surveying the plunder of the West by the uninvited.

'Fancy going in?' I said, caught up in the frenzy of the moment and looking at her in sudden elation. If there had been a cloud in the sky at that moment, it would have crossed her face. If a thunderstorm had exploded out of nowhere, it would have seemed only right and proper. Instead, her eyes went a shade darker and she looked at me in horror.

'I'm not going in there with them,' she said, sounding strangely like her mother. She sat down firmly on the cliff edge, which was really the bank of grass by the pool, to emphasize her decision. My mind swam with thoughts, loyalty to my cousin who, unbeknown to her, I worshipped, with brown eyes like a camel, an open door to join the gang, hair like golden honey, a Welsh singing voice, fag ends from the gutter, and all the time the boys shouted and yelled like men-serpents calling me, their Odysseus, to cross to their liquid island. The magic was too strong.

In seconds I had pulled off skirt, and blouse and vest, glad that I didn't have to wear a liberty-bodice like some girls I knew, and was in with them. Laughing they made room for me. Sheila stayed at the edge, looking away in disdain at my common behaviour, her nose pointed to the sun and mine dipped into the coolness of the blue water.

17

The Enraged Dragon and the Cornered Wolf

It was raining.

I looked out of Gran's open front door at No. 39, which she had left open because of the fireballs, even though there was no storm in the air, and gasped in horror as I saw a ball of nylon mac and flowered umbrella rolling down the street in my direction. Aunty Phyllis.

It had been some days since my swim in the Dingle and I knew, as sure as anything that this would happen. She had dragged me over the coals a few months before when I had stripped to my knickers to play *Bomba the Jungle Boy* - in my own house.

'There's no 'arm in a bit of fun, Sheila,' I had protested as we left the Dingle, 'no 'arm at all,' I added as we reached the top of the Common on the way home, and I struggled in vain to retrieve my right dap which had been sucked forever into the murky depths of a bog which had caught us by surprise.

Sheila had told. Before I could escape, Aunty Phyllis was filling the doorway, shaking the rain off her umbrella into my face and looking a grim shade of purple.

'Never, never,' she added, pushing me back into the room with the sharp point of her umbrella, 'in all my born days 'ave I been so ashamed, Bronwen Morrissey, as you 'ave made me.' I could hear Gran's ears pricking up behind me and fancied I felt the heat from her eyes drying the raindrops that were slithering down the back of my neck from Aunty Phyllis's disapproving umbrella. A thought made up of red and yellow flashes, the same colours as the flowers on the umbrella, fluttered under my eyelids. 'This,' it was saying, 'is what Hell must be like', with Aunty Phyllis in front and Gran behind, one bristling with the anger of an enraged dragon, the other as suspicious and ready to jump as a cornered wolf.

I was at a loss for words and could only take the barrage that bowled me over from the front door to the back face on.

'The 'ole town is talking.' I wanted to say that this was an exaggeration, because Gran, for one, hadn't heard about it, but I valued my life too much to give it up so stupidly, and Gran was told about it soon enough.

Saranne Morrissey (Gran) at front left with her sister Phyllis Eynon (Aunty Phyllis) at front right.

Dai and Stella Morrissey.

'And you 'ave got the cheek,' she said in a deathly tone, 'to go to Jerusalem on a Sunday. There is chapel for you.'

'Well,' went on Aunty Phyllis, 'it is alright for Miss Scarlet 'ere and 'er chapel, but I 'ave got to go to church and face everyone. What I shall say I just don't know! In 'er knickers!'

''er knickers!' repeated Gran, as if she hadn't just been told, 'and do your Dad know what you 'ave been up to madam?' I mumbled something to the effect that he was putting a television aerial up on the top of the Black Mountains somewhere. I shouldn't have said black, because now I was scarlet and black, scarlet as a harlot and black as sin.

'Of course, it is no use talking to 'er mother,' Aunty Phyllis said as if I was no longer there, 'the English do not know the ways of the Welsh.'

'I do 'ope,' said Gran, 'that she,' pointing a wavering, trembling finger in my direction in a manner that would have done any deacon proud, 'do learn from this, for there is nothing worse than a loose woman.'

Later that evening as I waited outside my father's garage, which he rented at the back of Plantation Street where the school canteen was, I rubbed my arms and legs all over to get rid of the remnants of the feelings of jelly and limp rags in them.

It was getting dark as Dad drove up to the garage. He gave me a wave, drove the car in, potched about for a bit, and then got out, slamming the door behind him. He lit a Players as he walked out to meet me.

''Ello, love,' he said.

''Ello, Dad,' I replied. 'Dad, what's an 'arlot?' When I told Mam what had happened, she went into a knot of laughter and I knew that Aunty Phyllis had been right; the English do not know the ways of the Welsh.

18

The Lucky Lump of Coal

'Well I'm off then, Gran,' I said, hanging around by the front door of No. 39 to give her a chance to remember. 'I'm going now then, can't be late for school today Gran, I'm sitting my 11+.'

'I don't know what you're making all the fuss for,' she said, not looking at me but pounding a bar of Lifebuoy heavily onto the shirt's collar she had spread across the scrubbing board in the bosh, 'you won't pass anyway.' My heart sunk to the floor, only she didn't see it and I ran out of the bailey and down lower Forge Street as fast as I could, only slowing down once I'd reached the start of Wellington Street.

The year before, Gran had given my cousin Sheila, Aunty Phyllis's girl, who was my second cousin really, a lump of black coal for luck at her exam and she had passed.

'Just do your best, love,' my mother had called back to me from the car that morning, 'you can't do better than your best,' and Dad had waved as the engine of his little black Austin, BUL 668, coughed into life and they had hiccupped their way up the street on their way to Hirwaun, where they worked at Sobell's. Mam worked on the lines with little coloured resistors and coils and things, and Dad was one of the bosses.

Well, I did try my best, but it was hard, especially when I seemed to finish much earlier than everyone else in my restricted 'look in front of you, girl, or live in disgrace for the rest of your life' vision. Mr Price kept looking at me with a concerned expression on his kind face. I knew that he was willing me to check my answers by the way he raised one shaggy eyebrow, then the other, and wiggled his dark moustache, or standing beside my desk, took his thick-lensed spectacles off, rubbing frantically at the clean lenses with a big, man's hankie which he kept in his top pocket but never used to blow his nose. Every time he took the hankie out of his pocket a cloud of chalk dust exploded in his face and the more he tried to shake it away the more it danced and teased and hovered in the air around him.

All the way through the exam a big empty space by the inkwell kept looking at me, the space where my lucky piece of coal should have been. I kept thinking of how much better I would have done if only it had been there.

Then I felt guilty and selfish because my twin, who had been ill for two years, was stuck in a bed in Sandbrook House Hospital at Merthyr Tydfil, instead of sitting at the desk next to me, doing his 11+.

Bernard Morrissey in 1958 aged eleven. He is photographed at Sandbrook House with Alan Brill who was also a patient there.

Just for him, I spent the last ten minutes doing the sensible thing, staring hard at every answer, changing them and putting them back again the way they were before. Mr Price and his cloud of chalk dust walked on.

My paper was a mess!

I sensed Mr Price's approach again behind me on his way back to lean over my shoulder. The smell of his pipe tobacco which clung to his tweed jacket always wafted ahead of him like a finger of vapour pointing the way. I heard him trying not to sigh, although a sound like a little puff of wind escaped and hit me on the back of my ear; my unruly hair being forced back with a metal clip. It wasn't until the following year at the new school I had to get it cut when I picked up lice.

He was used to my untidiness. Only two years before, just before our ninth birthday, hand in hand with my twin, I had been sent around each class in the school where we had to show our writing books to everyone.

Bernard was the good example and I was the bad one.

'This, children,' Miss Jones had said in a voice whose amplification belied her diminutiveness, 'is what good writing should look like,' and Bernard had squirmed in embarrassment at the front of the class, glancing at me in sympathy for what he knew was coming next. 'And this,' she said, holding out my book with the very tips of her fingers, as if it had been crawling with germs, 'is how NOT to write.' I glanced sideways at Bernard's perfect rounds, and curls and straight lines and then at my smudged blotty effort.

She had a point, but then, I was left-handed. My hand sort of smudged the ink as it moved across the page and the nibs on the pens I had were always split or bent, and my ink wells usually had blotting paper and other mysterious revolting matter stuffed inside them; stuff that looked as if it came out of noses. They should have been grateful for any writing at all really. Until I was eight I had baffled them all by writing completely in mirror writing, not just a 'p' or a 'b' in reverse like the infants. I even formed my own special club where all the members had to write the same way; I was the only one in it.

I held my head up, focusing my gaze on a print of Picasso's blue boy holding a dove, which was nailed on the wooden partition between standard four and five, stubborn

Group photograph taken inside the Wellington School, Rhymney. The partition between the classrooms can be seen. Brian Morrissey is third in from the right in the bottom row.

Mr D.T. Williams.

in the knowledge that I was the first one in my class who could spell 'immediately' and knew 'Daffodils' and 'Leisure' off by heart.

'What is this life if full of care,' I whispered inside my head, while Miss Jones rattled through her lecture with the speed and accuracy of a tommy gun spitting bullets. 'A poor life this if full of care we 'ave no ' She spat the last one and gave me that look, the one she used when I showed her my cross-stitch sampler, left-handed of course, with the stitches going the wrong way.

'Unpick it,' she would growl for the umpteenth time that day and I would return meekly to the back of the class where I belonged.

Mr Edwards had been in charge of the school until the new headmaster arrived. I liked Mr Edwards. He was a little man, or perhaps I should say short, for he did not give the impression of little, especially when he opened his mouth to speak, for he spoke in a rich baritone which reminded me of an actor reciting on a stage. I had never seen one but I imagined that all actors must speak like Mr Edwards. He wore thick horn-rimmed glasses and a smile upon his face whenever he passed me in the corridor with the corners of his check jacket flapping under the folds of his black gown and slapping of the wide legs of his fawn flannels, marching smartly of course.

It was the new headmaster who gave us the results of our 11+, Mr David Thomas Williams, Rhymney born and returned again to Rhymney after leaving Mynydd Bach, near Chepstow, to the care of someone else. Poor Mynydd Bach!

There were seven of us altogether, called to the headmaster's room and standing squashed in a line before his desk. Robert Jones with his dark curly hair and hand-knitted cardigan, whose mother gave piano lessons in a house near the cenotaph. She gave me a few lessons, in a manner of speaking.

''Ere is the money for your piano lesson, Bronwen.'

'Thanks Mam.' My mother, being English through no fault of her own, had high hopes of my becoming cultured as she saw it, which meant playing the piano, growing up to become a leggy and beautiful debutante, being presented to the Queen and then marrying Prince Charles as was the way of things. So every Saturday morning for some months or so I walked up to the little house near the cenotaph where Robert Jones's mother gave piano lessons, and every Saturday morning, just before I reached it, my brother, David, was waiting with his hand out to take the money for the matinee at the Scala.

'I don't think we'll bother with the piano lessons any more, love,' said Mam one day as she was listening to me practice,' there is a new dancing school opening up Carno Way, tap and ballet.' She put special emphasis on the word 'ballet'. I sighed inwardly and looked down at my extremely pigeon toes and two left feet.

'That's nice, Mam,' I said. David couldn't be bothered walking as far as Carno to trap me. He was busy with his friend Gwyn Griffiths and their newly formed skiffle group; this consisted of a large tea-chest that filled our kitchen and Gran's scrubbing board.

The Scala, High Street, Rhymney. (Photograph courtesy of Mr Norman Gilbert)

David Morrissey.

Some months later my mother was rewarded when I starred in two parts, one as a frozen snowman with outstretched arms in the dance school's production of *Winter Wonderland* and the other as a gallumping horse pulling the Snow Queen's sleigh.

Irene Baker, from Plantation Street, was another of the seven to pass her 11+ that year. She was the only girl in the class taller than me and the only one I ever had a fight with, over goodness knows what. I think I stood up to her gang when I shouldn't have, anyway, she hit me in the eye and I gave her a good bloody nose, having Irish blood in me from Merthyr.

There was little Carole Price, from Plantation, who only came up to my shoulder, with her nut-brown hair, parted like a ruler down the middle, and nut-brown eyes and a lucky gap between two front teeth which meant she would be rich when she was older. Russell Howells from Lady Tyler had passed too; all the girls loved him because he was a nice little boy with a sweet face. I think the others were Gareth Jones and Janice Llewellyn, Gareth tall and thin with white blonde hair and Janice, a shy, kind little mouse of a girl with a ribbon in her hair, and me, Bronwen Morrissey, from Forge Street, Dai Morrissey's youngest, who tore the ribbon out of her hair as soon as she reached the first corner in the street.

Group photograph taken in the playground of the Wellington School, Rhymney. Top row: Gareth Price fifth in from right, Robert Jones seventh in from right. Middle row: Bronwen (the author) is seventh from the right, Janice Llewellyn is second in from the right, Carole Price is first on the left, Dolly Walters is fourth on the left, and Irene Baker is sixth on the left. Bottom row: Noel Price fourth in from left, Dai Eynon seventh in from the right, Russell Howells fourth in from right. Teachers are Miss Hendry and Mr Price.

Mr Williams leaned back in his chair and surveyed each and every one of us with kind eyes looking out from under heavy eyebrows. I was glad his eyebrows didn't meet in the middle because Gran had told me that men like that were murderers.

'You have worked very hard,' he said, sounding posh to us with all his aitches, and speaking with that pleasing lilt that people have when their first language is Welsh, 'and I am proud of you all.' He said 'proud' like the purr of a cat and I decided I liked him there and then. 'I am sure that Wellington School is very proud of you,' he paused, lifting his empty pipe off the desk and placing it in his mouth for inspiration. I thought he looked like a poet and wondered if he had met Miss Jones yet and if she had shown him my cross-stitch sampler.

'You see,' he said, 'there are many things that make us what we are, and in Rhymney, it is coal and nonconformity and the Welsh language that have made us what we are.' We all shuffled uneasily for this was chapel language and 'the future is very important' language which we knew would fly over our heads. I didn't know what nonconformity was and most of Lower Rhymney had lost their Welsh somewhere along the line, except for swearing; my Gran could swear in Welsh.

'It was the schools see,' she had told me, 'put you in the corner with a dunce's cap on your 'ead if you spoke Welsh, or made you walk around the playground with a board 'ung round your neck. The only way to get rid of it was to tell on someone else if you 'eard them talking Welsh and the last one with the board round their neck at the end of the day 'ad the caning.'

Russell Howells didn't seem bothered, but then he was a Catholic, which was something else we didn't understand, only knowing that he had a special church of his own and didn't have to come to our school assemblies if he didn't want to, but could sit in a class on his own looking at library books. My Grancher had been a Catholic, having Irish blood from Merthyr Tydfil, but when he was away in the war and the priest had told Gran she had to wait for him to come back before my Dad could be splashed with holy water or something, she had marched to St. Matthew's in a temper and had him baptised there.

Coal we understood. We only had to look out of the window behind the headmaster's head to see the black patch in the distance, and the coal tips by the railway bridge on the bend to Pontlottyn. Probably every one of us had mining somewhere in the family. I stole a glance at Mr Williams. He had an awful knowing look about him and I wondered if he knew about Gran and my lump of coal.

So that was it, seven of us from the Wellington that year allowed to pass into a future world of academia, while the ones left behind started to think about the pits, Smith's factory and the Forge.

'It won't be so bad,' I told my friend Dolly Walters, who would be going to the Annexe, 'we can still be friends.' Dolly lived in upper Forge Street, No. 23, which was the corner house, where my side of the street was split in half by Jerusalem Street sticking its nose in, or foot I suppose, because it was the bottom of Jerusalem and not the top.

Dolly's house wasn't like mine. Her bailey wall was higher than a tall man. Not that there were many tall men in Rhymney, although Gran told me her father, Davy Jones, had been tall. I had seen a tall man once standing on the platform at Cardiff Central, his head and shoulders sticking up above everyone else. When I pointed him out Gran had laughed and said he must have come from North Wales, where the Welsh were taller. The path leading through the gap in the wall to Dolly's door found its way up in steep uneven steps, wobbling and cracking with the effort of the climb and the pushing away of the nettles that tried to uproot its stones.

We started off our friendship by playing ' 'ouse' in her back garden , where we gathered stones and laid them to make squares on the ground which were the rooms. Dolly found a chipped cup and I found an old saucepan without a handle so we could cook with mud and water. Every so often her mother would come out to the back garden, wiping her hands on her pinny, and have a look at what we were doing.

'Well , now, that do look a nice cake you are making girls, only make sure you do do it right, mix it a bit more now and do it tidy.' After some weeks, we spread our wings and headed off every day to the Works.

Behind the Forge were stacks of wooden pallets, piled sky high to little girls. We climbed up and up and up towards Heaven with all the treasures we had found;

The coke ovens in the ironworks at Rhymney. (Photograph courtesy of Mr Norman Gilbert)

White Welsh pony. (Photograph courtesy of Beth Wieland, www.scarboroughfarm.com, USA)

coloured glass, broken bits of china, smooth pebbles, soap-stones from the river, polished coal and chips of iron pyrites which was our gold. 'Fool's gold' Gran had called it. We made a house on the very top of the pallets and when Dolly wanted to go shopping, we climbed down and down and down, and then she pushed her pretend baby in a pretend pram along the grassy lane that was the roof of the old coke ovens in the ironworks.

I didn't push a pretend pram because I was a Welsh princess riding along on my snow white horse with its silver mane and its silver tail swishing like shining stars against a backdrop of blue sky.

Sometimes we went to the McLaren to stare at what was left of the old pit, craning our necks to look up at the arched windows and looking down in awe over the crumbling walls, which were taller than the height of two or three houses piled on top

Rhymney Ironworks, Old Middle Furnace Site.(Photograph courtesy of Mr Norman Gilbert)

of each other. We found rusty old pipes or old fence wires to use as ladders to get us to the bottom.

Once I found a wooden hatch over a hole in the ground. It took me ages to slide it off the hole but when I did I found myself staring into a blackness beneath me that was darker than any night. I dropped a stone down it, but although Dolly and I listened for ages we never heard it hit the bottom. I thought of the filled in mine-shaft higher up on the other mountain, where the old Duffryn was, and how we used to swim around its edge.

Then one summer, my cousin, Dai Eynon, Aunty Phyllis's boy, who was my second cousin really, had nearly drowned in it because he swam too close to the middle and could feel himself being sucked down. My big brother, David, had grabbed him by the seat of his trousers and pulled him out and we had slid him down the mountain on the big water pipes that ran down its side. Aunty Phyllis had gone wild when she found out.

'Better put the board back on it,' I said to Dolly. So we did.

But in the natural way of things, after the 11+, with her school on one side of Surgery Hill and mine on the other, in time we drifted apart, only smiling or waving from a distance whenever we caught a glimpse of one another.

The summer that followed my exam was a hot, hot summer. Dad decided to take me and Mam and Judy, our little dog, to North Wales. Brian, who lived with Gran

Brian Morrissey in army uniform.

and Grancher, was waiting to be called up for his National Service in the Army, Ann was married and David was away with the Air Force cadets. Bernard was still in hospital.

I remember it was that summer because that was the summer I came 'on', periods and menstruation not being words used at that time, which caused a lot of problems

David Morrissey in RAF cadet uniform.

David and Brian Morrissey.

with hiding things from Dad and furtive buying of 's.t's' from chemist shops, sanitary towels not to be said aloud. Mam said it was a pity with me being so young and not to go swimming or wash my hair when 'it' was happening.

'I 'ave got a friend in Cardiganshire,' said Dad as we set out, 'from the Air Force. 'e 'as always said we are very welcome to stay with 'im. Married a Welsh girl, lovely looking, couldn't speak a word of English.'

We found Cardiganshire without too much bother and Dad drove around the country roads and through little villages made up of two or three houses looking for his friend's house until, at last, much to Mam's relief and mine, he decided to stop and ask someone.

'Do you know where Billy John do live?' he asked, 'Married a Welsh girl who can't speak a word of English.' The old farmer, who couldn't speak a word of English, nodded and pointed us to a cottage sitting on the edge of a cliff which looked to be a few miles in the distance. It was getting dark by the time we got close to the cottage and then we couldn't find the road leading to it, so Dad drove across the fields and pulled up at the door just as his friend was coming out of it.

'Dai, mun!' he exclaimed in obvious delight. 'Well well, there is a lovely surprise. Come in, mun, come in Stella. Duw, Duw, you 'aven't changed a bit in all these years.' Mam giggled like a schoolgirl. 'And who is this lovely little girl?' I blushed.

To be fair to Dad's friend, he took us all into the house and got his wife to make us a nice cup of tea. I stared at her as she busied herself around the table in the one small room they had downstairs, and then looked at the four daughters sitting squashed together on a bench in the corner. The mother was as round as she was tall, her graying hair pulled back into a tight bun and some of her teeth were missing. The daughters, all slender and tall, had blue eyes like the sea on a cloudless day at Tenby, and long flowing golden hair the colour of Ceredigion corn.

'Pity I didn't know you was coming, Dai,' Dad's friend was saying, 'I'm on night shift see, but my wife will look after you, won't you love, and give you a bed for the night.' His wife didn't say a word. 'Can't speak English, see,' Dad's friend explained, laughing.

I looked around for a bed, and couldn't find one, but there was a set of wooden steps leading up to a floored space under the roof, just like the one I had read about in *Heidi*.

As soon as Dad's friend had gone, his wife shoved the table over and spread some blankets on the floor for us and without a word struggled up the wooden steps closely followed by her four daughters. In the morning she made us a cup of tea and some boiled eggs.

'Very kind of you,' Mam said, smiling prettily. 'Why don't you go outside and play with the girls, love?' she added turning to me. I went outside with Judy. The four sisters were standing on a tump near the edge of the cliff looking like some story out of the Mabinogian. As soon as they saw me approaching them they took to their heels and went racing away across the meadows. I watched them until their golden hair was but a shimmering speck in the distance.

'Bronwen,' shouted Mam in a funny sort of voice, 'we are going.' She all but shoved me into the car and Dad started the engine up. We hadn't even reached the end of the field before they started laughing so hysterically that the car swerved and Dad had to stop driving for a few minutes.

'What's wrong?' I asked incredulously. Mam couldn't speak. She was laughing too much. She handed me a dirty piece of torn paper. 'Bett and brecfast', it said, 'too shillins and eleven pens.'

19

The Rainbowed Soap Bubble

'She is going to be a teacher,' Mam said green eyes sparkling, elbows resting on the bailey wall and talking to Mrs Davies, from No. 35, as proud as punch. She had obviously forgotten the episode of Mrs Davies's giant of a mongrel who had scaled a high fence in the back garden and got at our little Judy, giving her three pups that nearly ripped her in half when they arrived. We gave one to Aunty Phyllis.

'What shall I call it?' she said.

'Call it Rip,' I suggested and Mam shot me a daggery look.

Rip was very fond of me. Every time I visited Aunty Phyllis at No. 16 Lady Tyler, she had to run for a mop because he piddled with excitement, leaving a snaky, slithery trail along the length of the passage. She had him for years and he always welcomed me in his own wet way.

'I don't know why the 'ell that dog do pee when you come 'ere,' she complained, mopping furiously on her knees and looking at me suspiciously. 'The dog do only do it for you.'

I shrugged my shoulders innocently and stole a secret glance at Rip, who was winking and smiling.

Mrs Davies was also looking as proud as punch because her son, John, had already been at the grammar school for one year and by all accounts was a very clever boy.

'I can tell you all about the Lawn,' she said, 'because my son, John, 'as been there for a year.' We already knew that of course, and Mrs Davies knew we knew it, but my mother having learnt well the ways of the Welsh, apart from laughing fit to bust when she heard about me swimming with the boys in the Dingle in my knickers, showed some surprise and admiration at the news.

'Well, isn't that good, Bronwen? Mrs Davies's son 'as already been there for a year and 'e can tell us all about it.' No sooner said than done. Before we could blink an eye John was called out to the bailey which he shyly approached with all the enthusiasm of a tortoise being dragged out of its shell. He politely answered a barrage of questions from my mother while I tried to look as apologetic as I could.

'John will show you round,' said Mrs Davies to enhance the conversation, and I don't know who cringed in horror most, me or poor John Davies. 'Well, well, so you do want to be a teacher?' Mrs Davies said, turning to me and smiling her approval.

Mam was giving me one of her looks, so I said,'Yes, Mrs Davies,' and left it at that, not bothering to mention that I had told Mam I wanted to be a vet. Mam had tossed her head back, laughing in her hearty way, and then seeing the look on my face stopped laughing and explained as gently as she could that only boys could be vets. It had annoyed me, the way I felt annoyed on Saturday mornings when Dad took Bernard to look at the factory, before he went into hospital, and I had to stay at home because I was a girl.

I was glad I hadn't told her what I really wanted to be, deep down, so deep down that it was a dream, and if I mentioned it, it would probably pop in the air like a rainbowed soap bubble and there would be nothing left but the memory of what it had looked like.

As it turned out I went to school on that first day with Carole Price, from Plantation, the one with the nut-brown eyes and lucky gap between her teeth. I called for her at her house in Plantation, proud as punch in my new navy blazer with *Honi Soit Qui Mal Y Pense* written large all over the breast pocket. My navy gymslip was resplendent with a girdle of red around its middle, the hem of which, the rules said, had to touch the ground when I went on my knees. I wore a red and navy striped tie, white ankle socks on my feet with no holes in the heels; red, knee-length and black stockings were for prefects and sixth-formers.

Gwyn Griffiths at the Forge, Rhymney.

I pulled my blazer back a bit to flaunt my Persil white blouse and rocked on my toes to squeak the black leather shoes, brand new from Pugh's on the corner in High Street. Every so often I threw my brown satchel made from real leather, which smelt like Tom the cobbler's in the Cutting, on and off my shoulder to highlight its poshness, and to top it all, my navy tam with a badge on it balanced precariously at a jaunty angle on my tawny nest.

''Ow do I look?' I had asked Brian outside No. 39.

'You're awful round-shouldered,' he said, 'stand up straight and stick your bust out.' I watched him as he ran along the street crossing the road to the Powell's house and cutting through it to the Forge.

Pulling my shoulders forward a bit more and slinking down another inch, I made my shuffling way towards Plantation, my face as red as a beetroot because Brian had noticed my blossoming chest and called it a 'bust'.

Carole opened the door. I stared at a mirror image of myself, only shorter, much shorter, and daintier, and prettier, and tidier, with no round shoulders or bust, and with eyes of discernable colour. Mrs Price was all smiles, and Carole's Aunty Mary took me to see her knitting machine, the likes of which I had never seen before, and showed me the many-coloured pastel scarves and jumpers she had made on it.

Carole's younger brothers laughed and gave us playful shoves and punches, and her twin brother, who was called Noel because they had been born on Christmas day, and who was going to the Annexe, smiled his toothy grin. Carole and Noel were the only twins I knew in Rhymney except for Richard and Margaret Oliver, who lived at the other end of Plantation. Richard was a nice boy who wore glasses, the sort of boy to make a good Clerk of Works when he grew up, or Mayor of Rhymney at a pinch.

Margaret was quiet, pale and freckled, but they were younger and would have to wait their turn for posh uniforms and photos and knitting machines.

That first day we were both put into form 1b, and even though I explained to Mam that 1a and 1b were the same she really didn't get over it until I had gone through 2a, 3a and 4a to restore her pride a bit, and safely reached the status of fifth form.

Richard Oliver in Plantation Street, Rhymney. (Photograph courtesy of Susan Oliver, Rhymney)

There were three school houses for sports, competitions, eisteddfods, wars and the like. I was in Morgannwg which had a blue badge, and Carole was in Brycheiniog which was red. Green was for Gwent.

Doris Short, the Welsh teacher, who really was short but didn't let it bother her, and who had piercing blue eyes, taught us the Lord's prayer in Welsh, the Welsh National Anthem and Ierusalem, which was the school song, all in the first week.

'Mam,' I said that weekend, 'next year we can learn Welsh or French. Can I do Welsh?' David had done Welsh with Miss Short for four years. In his final exam she had given him one mark out of a hundred for getting his name right.

'No indeed!' said Mam, 'you are not learning any language I don't understand. Anyway, one day you might go to France.' Pigs might fly to the moon!

'But Mam, you can't speak French either.'

'That 'as got nothing to do with it.' Strange and stubborn, the reasoning of the English.

So when the time came I took French, the teacher being Miss Dilys Price, who we called Noddy because she nodded her head as she spoke. She worked us hard in a French sort of way, flashing her big forget-me-not blue eyes and fluttering her long velvet lashes. We repeated faithfully what she said in a cloud of self-consciousness. The room rattled with French words bouncing up to the ceiling and down to the floor and up again on the soft sing-song of accents made for Welsh intonation and we struggled to fit French onto our tongues while the bruised remnants of Welsh in our brains squeezed ever backwards into secret niches, to be smothered along with the pressures of dunces' caps, boards around the neck and Education Acts made at Westminster.

I told Carole my dream.

'Don't laugh,' I said as we sat on the corner wall, at No. 24, where Mrs Magnus lived, our feet dangling into the foot of Jerusalem. 'But I do want to be a writer when I grow up.' She didn't laugh. 'And a poet,' I added, testing her loyalty to the utmost. She passed the test, and the two of us clung together for the next four or five years until she left school to be grown-up and get work and marry, and I didn't, not until a long time after anyway.

20

Happy Teens

Across the road and up a bit from the cenotaph was a garage called Fosters, which had a small café attached to it.

I was in there with Carole one day after school, as was our usual way of things, drinking our Vimtos and playing Neil Sedaka's 'Oh Carol' on the jukebox over and over again and talking about our latest crushes. I had never heard of a song with my name in it, although I always sang 'My Bonnie lies over the ocean' with Bernard as a party piece when we were little, and I was sometimes called Bonnie by my mother.

'Isn't she bonnie!' someone would say, meaning chubby I suppose, then there would be a momentary pause for effect , and as I cringed, Mam's face would light up and out it would come, her cockney accent returned in full flow in the excitement of the moment.

'That's 'er name!'

The site of Foster's Garage, Rhymney. (Photograph courtesy of Robin Drayton)

Carole was quite keen on the new chemistry master whose name I can't remember, but he came from Durham, wore a tweed jacket which had the same tobacco aura as Mr Price from the Wellington, and walked around with his pipe in his mouth at a rakish angle. I liked Eric Smith, the biology teacher and a pimply red-headed boy in our class, whose surname was the same name as one of my pet prize rabbits, of which I had many, being the proud owner of rosettes and certificates won at competitions held upstairs in the Puddlers' Arms in Moriah Street, which was around the corner from Forge Street. Anyway, this boy had the same name as one of the Blue Beverans, although I really preferred the Silver Foxes.

The door opened and Lynda Moseley, from Abertysswg, who was very attractive in an Italian sort of way, her grandfather being Italian and having a chip shop in the High Street, came in with a few more of the Abertysswg crowd along with Elizabeth Sutton, from Tredegar, whose father had a newsagent shop on the Circle by the town clock.

''ave you two 'eard,' she asked, 'that the Shows are 'ere.' I was busy being jealous over her lovely blue eyes, cornflower, but Carole nudged me in excitement and we followed the others outside, climbed the grass bank beside the garage and wondered how we could have missed the hive of activity buzzing so noisily in our proximity.

It was a hot, hot September and all that week, Nesta Bell Richards, our Art teacher, who had frenetic sandy-red hair and was spotted all over with freckles and paint, took us onto the grass bank to sketch the goings on. We tried to sketch the dodgems because that was where the best looking show boys were, and when the Shows were up and going proper, I wore my new minstrel striped trousers and shocking pink socks, because I was going through my rainbow stage, and Carole wrapped a chiffon scarf around her neck. We shamefully ogled the men and boys as they leapt and darted from one dodgem car to another, flashing their gypsy smiles and sleeking back their

The Town Clock, Tredegar. (Photograph courtesy of the webmaster@tredegar.co.uk)

The Puddlers Arms, Rhymney. (Photograph courtesy of Robin Drayton)

The Lawn House, Rhymney.

long strands of black oily hair. We never got anywhere of course, not even a free ride on the dodgems.

I didn't seem to have much success with boys, blaming it partly on my best friends who were always better-looking than me and cared about things like fingernails and powder puffs and pretty clothes. There had been Delme Davies, from Abertysswg, when I was fourteen or fifteen, asking me out indirectly through a friend; fifteen to tell the truth.

'Do you want to go out with my friend?'

'Why don't 'e ask 'er imself?' my friend said on my behalf. I peeped over her shoulder to see a boy in the distance peeping over the shoulder of another boy.

We went out twice I think. I know it is shameful to say I think, because a first date is always to be remembered, but that is the way of it and I am sorry. Once we went to Tredegar, where we kissed in a lane behind the shops. I didn't really know how to, although I think Delme didn't do too badly. The other time we went for a walk in Rhymney where we ended up, against our own inclinations, running full pelt down a tip by the cemetery in the dark and would have, no doubt, been killed but for Delme's quick action of sitting us both down on the ground, where we slithered and rolled and tumbled all the way to the bottom, just stopping short of the river. He limped me home to No. 36.

It killed the romance though and I had grass and coal stains on my new white jeans which wouldn't wash off.

'Disgusting!' Gran said.

'I do 'ope you are ashamed of yourself,' said Aunty Phyllis looking at my belly for signs.

'Nothing 'appened!' I insisted. Gentlemen, the boys of Abertysswg.

The following year a group of us were sitting in a circle around a table in a room in Treorchy House. Treorchy House served as school library and had a good look-out point upstairs; it was the domain for music rooms and 'up to no good' senior pupils who were allowed a room downstairs.

Our activities had already been interrupted once that morning by the approach of shuffling feet and the sound of someone, who we knew to be Mr Richards, the music master, humming Puck's song from *A Midsummer Night's Dream*. As was usual in such emergencies and with 'Where the bee sucks, there suck I' getting closer and closer, we all crammed into the very large music cupboard in the corner of the room and held our breath as Mr Richards turned the handle and entered the room. We heard his feet making straight for the corner and the cupboard. Before we could blink, he had opened the cupboard door wide and was staring at us, his kind old face just like Santa's without the beard.

'In a cowslip's bell I lie,' he sang softly through his teeth, reaching in through the sea of frozen faces and arms and legs and upside down torsos to pick up a manuscript which he placed carefully into his briefcase. He closed the cupboard door and in the darkness we could hear him shuffling off down the corridor, still humming his tune. When we were sure that all the cowslips and bees had gone we clambered out again.

''as anyone ever tried a ouija board?' asked somebody and in the true manner of the Welsh, without even thinking, it was no sooner said than done, for the light was out, the curtains drawn and a chair placed under the handle of the door.

The War Memorial. (Photograph courtesy of Robin Drayton)

'Is there anybody there?' asked Jennie from New Tredegar. YES the paper cup on the table spelled out and our fingers placed on top of it whizzed backwards and forwards across the table as the cup moved to each letter.

'What shall we ask it?'

'Ask it where it do come from.'

'And its name.' The questions started flying thick and fast and just as thick and fast the cup flew across the table, our fingers scrabbling like mad in the air to keep up with it, or I should say 'she', for it turned out to be a lady who had lived in the big house by the park. Then we got on to the more interesting stuff, about boys and our futures. At long last it was my turn. I got straight to the point.

'Will I marry a Welshman?' NO. Horror of horrors and a gasp of sympathy from the others around the table, because Bronwen Morrissey, of Forge Street, was going to marry a foreigner. 'Where will I live?' I asked, looking desperately for clues. GERMANY.

'I think,' someone said kindly, 'that you 'ad better not ask any more questions.' She asked the next and we all burst out laughing because the lady from the house by the park said that the girl near the window was going to have a baby in the spring.

'Load of rubbish!' we said. I was secretly glad because I didn't want to marry a foreigner and live in Germany.

'Look on the bright side,' someone piped in, 'at least 'e probably won't be English.' Someone rattled the door handle and we jumped into action.

'Who put this chair be'ind the door?' one of us said in a loud surprised indignant voice. The said chair was removed and Irene Baker walked in grinning all over her face.

Rhymney High Street. (Photograph courtesy of Robin Drayton)

'I 'ave just been to the bakery girls,' she said, 'who do want a jam doughnut?'
That day, after school, I met my mother by the cenotaph which was just outside the gate.

She was going to Thelma's to get her hair permed. I told her about the lady who lived in the house by the park and she went all serious, telling me that a lady had indeed lived in that house.

'Come on, Mam,' I laughed, 'you don't really believe in all that rubbish? If you do, I'll end up marrying a foreigner and living in Germany.' We were both bent double with laughing by the time we reached Pugh's shop on the corner in the High Street. The girl who had been sitting by the window in the room in Treorchy was gazing wistfully at the display in the shop window. She caught sight of me, half-smiled, and blushing, raced off guiltily around the corner.

'Who was that?' asked Mam, 'one of your friends?' I didn't answer. I was staring hard at the display of pink and blue and white and yellow, frilly, lacy, ribbony baby-clothes in the window.

21

A Baby in Ebbw Vale

'Come on,' Dad shouted, more excited than I had ever seen him in my life, 'we are going to 'ave a baby.'

'In Ebbw Vale,' I added grinning, and he laughed because he knew I was teasing him about the time when my twin and I were born.

'Not so much snow this time though,' he replied, 'and not so far to go.' It had come as a surprise to all of us when Mam told us she was having a baby, not least of all to her, because she was a big woman and didn't really find the bump until it was almost time. She was delighted, of course.

I wondered what it would be like having Mam at home. She had worked at Sobell's since Bernard and I started school at the age of five, and had been promoted from coil-winding to Coil Bay Inspector.

Dai Morrissey and his Singer Gazelle car.

'Well, well,' said Gran,' and there is your sister married with a baby of 'er own, and Brian in the army , and David in the air force and like to get married before we know it, and you and Bernard fifteen. Well, well!'

'Your Mam and Dad should know better,' said Aunty Phyllis, 'at their age. I do 'ope they are ashamed of themselves.'

I gazed over at Dad who was now clearing the snow from the bonnet of his car, a shapely Singer Gazelle, and doing his Stan Laurel impression at the same time. He didn't look ashamed.

'Let's go!' he shouted and was almost away without me, the car skidding round the corner into Jerusalem like a take of the Welsh Keystone cops.

I waited outside St.James hospital in the car, not being allowed in by the matron who was a dragon.

It was a boy.

''Ow is Mam?'

'Fine.'

'Did you call 'im Adam?' I asked, which had been my choice of name from some book or other, or it might have been because of Adam Cartwright in *Bonanza* on the television.

'Jonathan,' he replied, 'Jonathan Adam.'

''As 'e got dark 'air?' I asked, hoping for dark because it was lucky and thinking of all the midnight bells on New Year's Eve and how a boy with dark hair and a lump of coal could make his fortune in the Valleys going around the houses with the magic words ''appy new year and please for a new year's gift.'

'Fair.' He noticed my disappointment. 'But I think it will turn dark.'

'What colour are 'is eyes?' I asked, hoping for indiscriminate.

'Blue.'

'Ah well!' I sighed.

Stella Morrissey holding baby Jonathan at the front door of No. 36 Forge Street, Rhymney, February 1963.

'Well let's get 'ome,' said Dad, 'and tell them all the news. I'm dying for a nice cup of tea.' Dad started the car's engine, chatting nineteen to the dozen about Mam and my new baby brother. He promptly drove straight into the lamppost in front of the car.

I looked at him scathingly and he went into a fit of giggles just as three nurses came running up to the car to see if we were okay.

'Are you alright?' they asked in great concern as they opened the car door and looked at Dad who was still laughing uncontrollably.

'I'm alright,' I said, 'but my father might 'ave bumped 'is 'ead.'

'Poor dab,' they said, pulling him out of the car and steering him towards the hospital.

'Did 'e say if 'e was 'urt?'

'Well, 'e said something about dying.' Dad gasped for breath and looked at my face in disbelief, his wide-opened eyes rolling in his head. Trying to plead with the nurses he went in to another hysteric fit of laughing.

'It's alright, lovely,' I heard one of the nurses say, 'it is just an old knock on the 'ead.' Awful sympathetic the nurses of Ebbw Vale. As they pushed Dad with difficulty through the door I heard his voice.

'I 'ave just 'ad a baby see,' he explained.

'There, there,' said one of the nurses, 'you'll be as right as rain in no time.'

'In Ebbw Vale,' I whispered, smiling to myself in the dark. I turned away from the hospital window where Dad was trying to press his face against the glass and mouth something to me. I couldn't quite make it out, something about 'rugger' I think.

It was a clear November night, the snow pure and crisp on the car park grounds and walls, the stars twinkling in the sky over Ebbw Vale. In the distance I could see the stars over my own town of Rhymney. They were laughing at the joke I had played on Dad and sharing the joke with the people in the streets and houses who moved and breathed and lived and hoped and dreamed, like me, beneath a Valley sky.

Jonathan Adam Morrissey.

Other titles published by The History Press

Growing Up in a Welsh Valley: Sunshine on the Mayfield

BRONWEN HOSIE

This compendium of nostalgic tales about Dai Morrissey, the author's father, as he grows up in the Rhymney Valley will bring both tears of joy and sadness to the reader. It starts at the end of the First World War when Dai was four years old, and continues through his childhood years, to when he was a young adult leaving the mines and starting his own business. This book captures wonderful memories of family life, hilarious adventures with friends, and the sadness Dai felt on losing others in the pit.

978 0 7524 4756 8

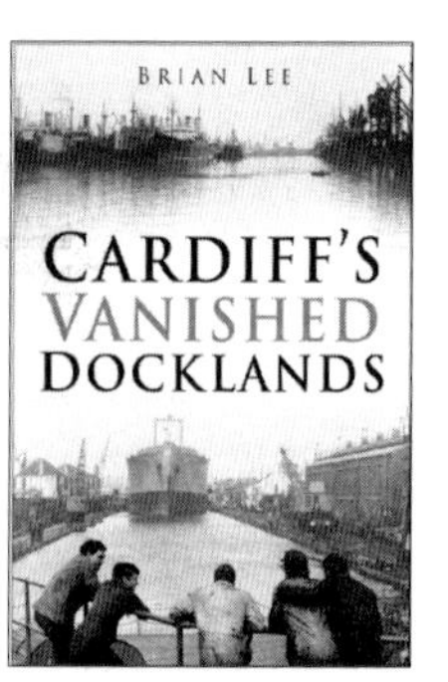

Cardiff's Vanished Docklands

BRIAN LEE

By the late nineteenth century Cardiff was the largest coal-exporting port in the world. This success brought with it immense industrial expansion. It wasn't until the 1960s and '70s, though, that major dock closures began in earnest. This decline produced massive areas of post-industrial wasteland – and in 1987 the Cardiff Bay Urban Development Corporation began to regenerate the docks. With the aid of over 300 photographs, Brian Lee tells the fascinating tale of Cardiff's docks, focusing especially on the people who worked here.

978 0 7509 4424 3

Cardiff: a Century Celebration 1905-2005

JOHN O'SULLIVAN AND KEVIN JONES

This title combines significant stories from every year of the century with personal memories of the city from its famous children and freemen to create a celebration of the Cardiff in words and pictures. In 2005, Cardiff celebrated two special birthdays - 100 years since it was made a city and 50 years since it became capital of Wales. This title combines significant stories from every year of the century with personal memories of the city from its famous children and freemen to create a celebration of the Cardiff in words and pictures.

978 0 7509 4181 5

Rhondda Revisited

EMRYS JENKINS AND ROY GREEN

This absorbing collection of old images offers a nostalgic glimpse into the history of the Rhondda Valley during the last century. Many aspects of everyday life are featured, from schools and churches, public houses and shops – the double-decker buses taking the workers to Alfred Polikoff's and local sporting derbies between Treherbert and Treorchy are also featured – to the carnival bands, the Saturday matinees and the local residents who have proudly called the Rhondda their home.

978 0 7524 3388 2

Visit our website and discover thousands of other History Press books.

www.thehistorypress.co.uk